The New University

Published by 404 Ink Limited
www.404Ink.com
@404Ink

Editing: Heather McDaid & Laura Jones
Typesetting: Laura Jones
Cover design: Luke Bird
Co-founders and publishers of 404 Ink: Heather McDaid & Laura Jones

Print ISBN: 978-1-912489-36-7
Ebook ISBN: 978-1-912489-37-4

Printed and bound in Great Britain by Clays Ltd, Elcograf S.p.A.

404 Ink acknowledges support for this title from Creative Scotland via the Crowdmatch initiative.

LOTTERY FUNDED

The New University

Local Solutions to a Global Crisis

James Coe

Inklings

This book is dedicated to all of my friends, colleagues, and former colleagues at Liverpool Guild of Students, NUS, and University of Liverpool whose work made me believe that universities can do brilliant things in the places they are based.

To my Liverpool friends who have kept my feet on the ground when my opinions far exceeded my ability.

And of course, to my fiancée Jess who made this book and all things in our life possible.

Contents

Introduction

If you've picked up this book the chances are you already have an interest in universities, education, or the social impact of such institutions. You might be one of the 2.5 million students in the United Kingdom[1] who are taking undergraduate, postgraduate, or doctoral study, from The University of Aberdeen in Scotland to the University of York in England, studying a whole range of subjects from Accounting to Zoology. You might be one of the thousands of non-academic staff who are maintaining estates, running outreach activities, administering programmes, sorting finances, building partnerships, or managing projects. Equally, you could be one of the 200,000 plus[2] full-time equivalent academic staff who are researching, teaching, and administrating (often all at once).

I write this book as one of those non-academic staff members. Every day in my job as a senior policy advisor at the University of Liverpool, I spend my time thinking about how my university can respond to policy challenges, embrace new opportunities, and do well by its students, staff, city, and wider region. Fundamentally, I believe universities are a force for good in the world and I do not believe this view is unusual. Liverpool is, for me, not just a place but it is *the* place that shaped my whole adulthood. Entry to the University of Liverpool gave me access to the place where I met my best friends, the city where I got my first job, and the qualifications which have made an enormous difference to my life. Such a difference that I now work at the university where I studied, and in some small way I hope get to give back to an institution to which I owe an awful lot.

Even from this description you will hopefully get a sense that universities are more than places that teach and carry out research. At their most basic, they give people skills codified into a degree certificate which they exchange for salary, opportunities, and experience. There is also a load of research behind the scenes which is carried out into indescribably vast areas of work. All with the intention of pushing the boundaries of human knowledge. Sometimes a university education has distinctly practical applications, sometimes it is purely to stretch our understanding of the world, and sometimes it falls somewhere in between, where the world may one day be able to use the more theoretical research.

My story is only one of millions, my institution is only one among hundreds, and, together, this life-changing impact with social consequence can do incredible good. It is this term 'community' which sits at the heart of everything I am interested in. To reduce the perception of universities to just teaching and research alone is to reduce the immense value they bring to their respective communities. I am also particularly interested in how much of that shapes the universities we have in the UK today. This is at the root of *The New University* and, by the end, we'll have a clearer idea of community's true place in the higher education system.

Even if you have not been to university yourself, it's likely that someone you know has – a relative, friend or colleague, perhaps. 97% of mothers, for example, regardless of whether they went to university themselves, want university education for their children.[3] The majority of chief executives of the UK's top 100 businesses attended university,[4] and every Prime Minister of this century attended university. By global standards, the UK significantly outperforms in higher education participation relative to its size,[5] and it is home to 18 of the world's top 100 universities[6] (if rankings are your thing). Their annual collective income is more than £40 billion per year,[7] and some estimates suggest they are stimulating £95 billion of further economic activity.[8] Whether you are aware of it or not, universities reach into every part of our economic, public, and social lives. They are the machines shaping our leaders, the engines driving the employment conditions of hundreds of thousands of people, and the anchors transforming the places they are based.

The New University is born from an urgent need for universities to claim a greater stake in our shared future as forces for social good – locally, nationally, and internationally. COVID-19 has brought this urgency into even sharper view as the sector charts a new purpose in the face of economic precarity, the threat of widening social inequalities, and in some quarters, questions of its very value. In spite of these challenges there is a positive future for universities to grasp and to shape. One where they are widely valued as forces for good; as vehicles for transforming lives through education; as magnets for jobs and opportunity; and, as always, open to change and in turn seen as legitimate in changing society. Rather than solely defending the value of universities here (after all, there are mission groups, hundreds of university public affairs staff, and a handful of excellent think-tanks, websites, and companies, who dedicate all of their professional energies to making sure universities get a fair hearing), I am interested in addressing a different question.

How can our universities do better in doing good by their students, communities, country, and society, in the post-COVID era?

In unpacking this question, it's necessary to know that not everyone sees the work of universities as a social benefit. Open up any national newspaper today and you'll find a story about universities and 'cancel culture'. A cursory Google search brings up moral panics about lecturers being warned for having opinions, universities being threatened with defunding if they do not protect freedom of speech, and a slurry of articles about students and students' unions disinviting (or often choosing not to invite) controversial speakers. This was most forcefully put forward by David Davis MP in introducing his motion for a Freedom of Speech (Universities) Bill[9]:

'Today, there is a corrosive trend in our universities that aims to prevent anybody from airing ideas that groups disagree with or would be offended by. Let us be clear: it is not about protecting delicate sensibilities from offence; it is about censorship. We can protect our own sensibilities by not going to the speech. After all, nobody is compelled to listen. But when people explicitly or indirectly no-platform Amber Rudd, Germaine Greer, Peter Tatchell, Peter Hitchens and others, they are not protecting themselves; they are denying others the right to hear those people and even, perhaps, challenge what they say.'

The word 'indirectly' is doing a lot of heaving lifting here. Amber Rudd had an invitation withdrawn by a student society, not a university; Germaine Greer actually spoke at Cardiff University; a member of private organisation the National Union of Students chose not to speak with Peter Tatchell; and Peter Hitchens would not agree to the University of Liverpool's Policy and Code of Practice Regarding Freedom of Speech, so spoke to the same audience ten minutes from the University premises. There was an event postponed by University of Portsmouth students' union that Hitchens chose not to reschedule. This is hardly the 'corrosive trend' Davis speaks about.

These examples are plainly a stretch, but they speak to a wider sense that universities are somehow different and separate from the society in which they operate, as secretly political institutions with an education wing attached. Almost entirely anti-Brexit, internationalist, and filled with those experts we supposedly no longer need, universities might be seen to have lost the cultural wars, finding themselves unmoored between their homes as liberal institutions and a government and media who have declared a 'war on woke'.[10] Even so, how can it be the case that it is clearly felt to be profitable political ground to criticise the places where such a huge portion of the population are educated, or employed? A sector which in the most basic terms employs more people than agriculture, forestry and fishing combined,[11] yet enjoys little of their political and public support.

Dismissing these criticisms of universities may make us feel better, knowing that we're right, or that it is at least governmental meddling yet again. However, universities will not reach the communities they were built to serve without reflection on how this scepticism came to be and how the sector might combat it. A clear analysis means facing up to where the sector has failed to bring the public with it and acknowledging perceptions may only change where it tackles some truly enormous challenges. Supporting the creation of good jobs. Being more effective vehicles for opportunity. And enhancing the prospects of the locations they are based.

To be robust in talking about universities should not mean dismissing the concerns about them. There is trap that public sector advocates fall into time and time again, telling people they are wrong through data, spreadsheets, and dispassionate economic analyses. This will not change their mind on deeply held beliefs. *The New University* aims to forge a new way for universities to *show* their value, not just tell people about it.

This might not be enough for some readers, and some might still be sceptical of a university's value. You may remember a time when you could leave secondary school, work in a stable job for your whole career, buy a home, enjoy holidays abroad, and do so from the strength of work experience and technical education without any university intervention. You might believe that only a certain type of higher education is valuable, and it's time to end 'mickey mouse' degrees. You might question why so many people should get to attend university, you will certainly see that question asked on your television.

For the MPs, newspapers, or the coterie of celebrities who never went to university and it didn't do them any harm, this refrain rarely includes their own family. In a world where there is an enormous gap between attendance in higher education for children who received free school meals and those who did not, reducing access will harm the poorest students the most.[12] There should be better technical provision for those who would benefit, and, yes, not every job should be ringfenced for graduates, and nobody is arguing that graduate employment is not important. However, for the country, society, and for everyone who wants a better life for them and their family, more education is an overwhelming force for good. Our task is not to turn back the clock but to face a reality that, for most, education is a key to a better life.

At the time of writing in 2021, as we confront the greatest public health disaster of modern times, and a deficit that governments will insist the nations pay off over a whole generation, we must pause to consider what universities can do to shape the 'new normal'. At a time when the country is relying on the research of universities to develop vaccines, the labour of student healthcare professionals to prop up our creaking healthcare system, and the collective will of society to pull together to save lives, it is incumbent on all of us who believe in higher education to take what we have learned now to build a better future for all.

COVID-19 will define the fabric of our society for generations to come. As the scale of the calamity unfolded, we saw some of the best of what our universities can do. We saw institutions give up their estate for nurses, students graduate early to get on to the NHS frontline, millions of pounds of funding diverted to COVID research, new engagements with civic partners to share expertise to save lives, and the wholesale mobilisation of digital technologies to keep teaching going. Of course, none of this has been perfect, without challenge, or error by universities themselves. But, instead of looking ahead with hypothetical problems, or a view to going back to 'how things were before', the pressing question of every policy maker should be what universities' actions during COVID can tell us about their capacity to teach, reach, and research in new ways to advance a more inclusive and prosperous society. The reason that there is so much passion about universities within the sector is because of their potential to do well. Every time an institution feels remote it is someone in their community who could feel the university is not for them. Every process or form might be necessary for those on the inside but for those looking to gain access to further education it presents a needless barrier. This book does not seek to tackle the huge discussion of tuition fees but amidst the debate of value for money our sector often has to prove its worth – it should be the *values* that are considered and not just its *value*. This has to be a relentless focus on opportunity, local impact, and shaping the economy through research. No university, and indeed no sector, is perfect, but that shouldn't stop our institutions doing their best with what they excel at, such as making a real difference to people's lives – exactly as they have sought to do during COVID-19.

The world is never going to be the same. If universities are to live up to their promise, they should never be the same either.

Chapter 1:
The Crisis of Work

Scour any popular student forum and you'll find students are deeply reflective, worried and excited about their futures. It could be said that they actually reflect on their motivations in much more nuanced ways than those who measure a university education by its economic value. The belief that the social utility of a university lies in pushing the boundaries of knowledge, imbuing a life-long love of learning, and engaging in the acquisition of knowledge purely for the pleasure of doing so, is perennially balanced against the value of higher education measured by its economic value, its capacity for preparing graduates for work, and the return on the investment of tuition fees.

Students are passionate about the courses they are going to study, nervous about what the future might hold, unusually terrified of being stuck in an office, and they want to get a great job. In short, their hopes for the future are like everyone else's. For those who have perhaps fallen short on their grades, been unable to go, or for hundreds of other reasons have decided not to go to university this year, there is a lot of understandable angst. Of course, reading these forum messages during 2021 offers a snapshot in a very tumultuous time so who knows what may happen in their academic lives in future, but these hundreds of personal stories set out a deep anxiety and active worry of who they believe to be 'in' and who is 'out'.

This is not surprising – who can blame them in the context of the COVID-19 fallout? Like many of us, they feel an acute anxiety about job opportunities. Work by the Higher Education Policy Institute found that while the majority of students were confident in finding a graduate job, the most commonly cited feeling on the process of getting a job was 'anxiety'.[1] In tandem with a decline in the availability of part-time work in bars, restaurants, and other traditional student term-time jobs, students are anxious about work and less experienced in it than the cohorts before them. This generation even have their own label: Generation COVID.[2]

These considerations are not only for personal misfortunes but they also ask profound questions about the role of higher education in, and after, economic crises. If university is anything, it is an implicit agreement between the state, students, and universities, that by undertaking further study a student's life will be better than if they had decided not to. Historically, universities have ameliorated work anxieties with skills development, careers coaching, advice, networking, and mentorships. These all still have a role, and will likely even have an enhanced role, but alone they do not address the central issue that there are more graduates than ever and a finite number of graduate jobs. This dynamic is only exacerbated by a profound economic shock like COVID-19 where a growth in university applicants and a contraction of the workforce is possible, if not likely. Only time will tell.

When it comes to graduate employability, the sector is therefore dealing with three separate phenomena today. The first is the employment of young people generally and the extent to which the market rewards them for their skills. The second is the capacity of the economy to absorb a growing number of graduates. The third, and perhaps the less explored, is the ability and desire of universities to create jobs through where they spend their money, time, and where they place their assets.

It is in this final bundle of activity that universities might make a real difference. They cannot ignore the waves of the economy, but for the places they are based and the students they teach, they might just build a life raft.

Is university worth it?

Ever since that day in Bournemouth in 1999 when Tony Blair set out to get 50% of young adults into higher education[3] there has been an often-repeated mantra that there are some people who shouldn't be going to university, and that they are studying subjects that aren't worthwhile. In recent years, this has been repeated by those sympathetic to the sector, who believe there needs to be more options other than universities,[4] and those who believe that universities are funnelling potentially skilled workers into unprofitable degrees.[5] There is nobody, absolutely nobody, making the case that *everybody* should go to university. However, if you begin from the premise that too many people are going to university, then you have to decide who shouldn't be 'allowed' to attend.

There is an approximate £9,500 annual wage gap between the median graduate and non-graduate salary.[6] This might be expected for high paying jobs where having a degree is a pre-requisite – for example, there is no debate about doctors, dentists or vets benefitting from a degree-level education. Equally, in the public imagination there are 'academics' who study in labs, or in experiments, or out in the field, and those feel like the type of activities that can only be supported in universities. There's also the cohort of people you might have grown up with – like your school teacher – who could be one of the few people you know personally who went to university. But what about all of those in-between programmes? The ones that further the value of human knowledge but don't directly link to a career but none-theless attract huge numbers of applicants every year. Those subjects that people study because they love it, because they are good it, because their parents said they should do it, or – *whisper it* – because they didn't know what else to do.

It turns out that these subjects also deliver a lot of personal and social benefit. Many of us will have heard the question 'what on earth are you going to do with x subject?' from friends and family. These barbs are often aimed at Arts and Humanities subjects, concentrated around media favourites like Media Studies (ironically enough), and part of conversations taking place with well-meaning parents and guardians who are often shelling out a lot of money in support and are worried about their child's debt. It's not unreasonable to ask if university is worth it, but context matters – a context found across surveys of students at all income levels who believed that their degree was useful to them.[7] We can also consider the facts against this questioning narrative: Arts and Humanities graduates make up the bulk of graduate employees in eight out of the ten fastest growing sectors of the economy.[8] And, to be personal for a moment, there are graduates like me who start a broad and interesting degree like English and learn a load of skills which help them in the future, even if their job is not directly related to their degree.

It's also impossible to prove that low-earning graduates would not have been even lower-earning without their degrees. Despite the mixed picture it's reasonable to suggest that, on average, there are distinct national and individual economic benefits to going to university. If the question is of rebalancing to different forms of education, that's fine, and in fact, an important conversation to be had, but it would be a national tragedy if the people who would benefit most from university are balanced away from it, and universities become even more exclusive in their attendance. As the Independent Schools Council, a representative body of 1,300 independent schools teaching more than 500,000 students, proudly boast, 91% of their students go on to university.[9] This compares to around 43% of state school students[10] (albeit this is likely higher for 21/22 but results were still being processed as the time of writing). It is therefore hard not to feel that those who talk about the alternatives to university never include themselves or their families in this equation.

'Worth' remains hard to pinpoint as a definitive 'yes, worth it' or 'no, not worth it'. There are plenty of jobs that require a university degree, deliver huge amounts of social benefit, but because of the nature of the economy do not return huge wages. Focussing on wages is not the same as a focus on value. In the context of COVID-19, nurses and other allied health professionals have been integral to relief efforts, yet do not command wages comparable to some of their peer group. It shouldn't be overlooked that when talking about graduate work, universities are only one element of the equation. Employers, be that public or private sector, paying adequate wages is an under-scrutinised part of the great university value debate.

Is university worth it *now*?

At the time of writing, young people have been through a once-in-a-lifetime financial crisis twice. The 2008 financial crash had a devastating impact on the whole labour market but particularly the employability prospects of young people. Equally, it is worth acknowledging that the country is still living with the impacts of the first financial crash today. By the end of 2011, almost 2.7 million people were looking for work; GDP did not recover for half a decade; it took 12 years for average wages to exceed pre-financial crisis levels; productivity still remains relatively low.[11] [12] The fallout from COVID-19 has a different origin. The ongoing economic downturn is being continually caused by the restriction of movement and its knock-on impact to business. However, there are echoes from 2008 that can still be heard today.

This will be a crisis where the pain is not evenly shared. Emerging statistics show that young people, the low-paid, and those from ethnic minority backgrounds are those most likely to be affected by COVID-19.[13] The long-term scarring on earnings for people who enter the labour market during financial downturns[14] is exacerbated for non-university leavers.[15] There may be worse to come. Emerging evidence suggests that the sectors that are in danger of shutting down employ large numbers of young people.[16] There are disproportionately large numbers of young people who were furloughed,[17] and there are fewer apprenticeships available than expected pre-pandemic.[18]

As independent think-tank Resolution Foundation summarise in their report *Growing Pains*:

'We find that people starting their careers in the midst of a downturn experience a reduction in real hourly pay of around 6 per cent one year after leaving education, and that compared to people who left education in better economic conditions their wages do not recover for up to 6 years. For those with lower levels of education, the chance of being in work falls by over 20 per cent, while for graduates the chance of being in a low-paying occupation rises.'[19]

Graduates are going to suffer severe economic difficulties but they will be less severe than those endured by their non-graduate counterparts. A report from the

Sutton Trust highlights that 39% of employers expect to hire fewer or no graduates while 27% anticipate they will hire more. 46% of graduates have said that the pandemic has had a negative impact on their graduate employability prospects.[20] According to research by Prospects, significant numbers of graduates are having existing offers of graduate jobs and internships and rescinded.[21] However, there was no reduction in the total number of graduates in work from the end of 2019 to the end of 2020.[22]

This could be because the impacts of COVID-19 have yet to be fully felt as government support schemes were still in full operation at this time. Another explanation for this could be that graduates are working in non-graduate jobs – around 47% of recent graduates were working in said non-graduate positions as of 2017.[23] As the Institute for Fiscal Studies point out in article 'A bad time to graduate', graduating in a recession is associated with working in lower paid and 'non-graduate jobs',[24] and also finding it harder to find both employment *and* well-paid employment. It is therefore reasonable to suggest that as demand for work shrinks, the supply could be filled by graduates entering non-graduate roles.

This is concerning for a number of reasons. For society, it's not good that access to meaningful employment should be confined to a specific demographic of the population, who have walked a specific path. Graduate employment also impacts the density of skills in a place. According to the Institute of Student Employers, London is home to the highest concentration of graduate jobs, and also the most desirable place to be a graduate.[25] Most cities are not retaining the majority of their graduates,[26] and there is a sense that particularly acute 'brain drain' carries professional talent away from towns to these more populous areas.[27] The economic crisis therefore brings a dual threat of graduates hoovering up non-graduate jobs, and also moving their labour to the few areas where they have a chance of securing a graduate job, and thereby reinforcing the competitive advantage of those areas – it becomes a self-fulfilling prophecy. This is more than a question about graduate retention – it is a question about how opportunity and prosperity is spread across the country.

None of this is to say that going to university isn't worth it even in the deepest of recessions. On a personal level, it is the ballast of career change and funded learning during the economic earthquake we are collectively living through. On a societal level, it is the chance for huge numbers of people to develop a broader range of skills as demand for work changes. There is surely no greater safety net to catch the fallout from COVID-19 than more people, with more skills, at a time where the future is so uncertain.

How can it be different?

In a world where the workforce is fractured, where single large employers play a diminishing role in our sense of place and national identity, and where automation and technological change will require both flexible labour markets and continual reskilling,[28] there is no single body who can divine future skills' needs. We are no longer living through the era of towns with single enormous employers be that heavy industry, ship yards, coal mines, or those former giant of British industry, British Leyland, Raleigh Bikes, or more recently BHS and Debenhams. Throw into this mix the disruption caused by often unstable 'gig' working where people are often, notionally, self-employed and reliant on unpredictable one-off freelance jobs to keep a roof over their heads, the ever-fragmenting workforce makes it an enormous risk to plan for today without thinking of what might come tomorrow.

There are two options.

1. Government can choose to believe that the role of employers and educators is to be buffeted by the economic waves and their function is to turn out students and employees who can meet the economic needs of today.

2. Government can empower businesses, communities, civic partners, and universities, as stakeholders in the economy which they shape and are in turn shaped by.

In a post-COVID world, there is a renewed need for universities to stimulate demand in the economy. Their role is not solely producing the supply side of skills, qualifications, and graduates. That is not going to be enough to build a brighter future for their students or their places.

This is not to say that skills development does not have a role. In fact, as the economy recovers, industry reopens and a new normal begins to settle, there will be a premium for graduates with a broad range of skills. It is the case that higher education can be both academic and vocational. Professional programmes, those like medicine and dentistry, combine an academic rigour but with a specific career path in mind. More broadly, it has been the business of careers departments, curriculum designers, students' unions, and others, to advocate employability skills within a student's learning. These roles will only become more important.

Universities as employers

Change should begin with what universities can most readily impact. Universities employ hundreds of thousands of people and support millions more jobs in their supply chains. In popular culture there is little exploration of university jobs beyond the caricature of the academic (usually a man) working on something brilliant that will change the world. In reality, the nature of the modern university is that it employs people with a huge range of skills. A large proportion of these are academics, but there are many careers available within the sector. There are jobs which you will find in any sizeable organisation, like HR, estates and finance; or academic-adjacent jobs like research support, or student-facing jobs like careers, alongside very specialised roles like technical and laboratory roles.

If those who are already in the most precarious employment are most impacted by economic downturns, then universities should strive to reach them first. There have too often been communities which are seen as 'too hard to reach', mirrored by a perception that universities are somehow different, aloof, or not the type of place they would consider working. Closing this perception gap can be a cornerstone of the new university. This means targeting recruitment differently, running advertisements outside of the usual places, and communicating why a university benefits from a breadth of talent.

This is a good start, but there is more the sector can do.

The COVID-19 pandemic gives universities the opportunity to consider where they are physically located and where having an open door to the community need not only be a metaphor. Running parts of university functions from shop fronts, offices, and units, across communities delivers some distinct benefits. It will allow universities to genuinely engage with the people whose lives they are seeking to change. Be that widening participation practitioners working in the communities they seek to recruit from, researchers basing themselves in the communities with whom they carry out research, or more generally the university having a permanent presence which brings it to life.

Universities are naturally impacted by the wider conditions in the economy. Like the businesses in their local areas, they will have to make difficult decisions to ensure they continue to deliver their core missions of research and teaching. However, they need not engage in this mission alone. As government looks at how places will be physically changed by COVID-19, the moment is ripe for a serious conversation with the sector on how capital expansion could be incentivised to give a boost to our towns and cities.

In the era of wider high street decline, this presents an opportunity for universities to genuinely play a part in the economic renewal of their places. In their purchase of a local department store, the University of Gloucester has stolen a march on this agenda. They have taken over a bankrupt store and committed to refurbishing the building. In bringing the building back to life they will provide teaching space and space for community activity. The beauty of this arrangement is that it gives the university space to grow and the city a tenant large enough to bring other services of community benefit in their space.[29] Increasing the footprint of the institution will also help spread its agglomerate benefit. These are the people who will move to be close to their office, the businesses made viable through people being nearby, and the industries which pop up because they want to be near institutions. There is no sign that demand for universities is slowing down, so this should not be a full dismantling of estates, which itself would bring issues, but a concerted effort to spread prosperity.

If the challenge is around jobs in the sector's own institutions, it is also about where universities choose to spend their money. Organisations like the Civic University Network and Preston Council have advocated for the principles of community wealth building.[30] [31] Amongst other measures this model advocates that institutions, like universities, should use their position to retain funding locally so it can be used for social benefit. This can be done through fair employment practices, local procurement, and giving local people a greater say over how their institutions work with their places.[32] Universities, by their nature, purchase a lot of goods and services. The more that their money is used to support local economies, the more will flow into local employment, and the more they can address some areas of long-term economic harm.

Research by the Higher Education Procurement Association found that universities are procuring more than £7.7 billion worth of goods, of which around a third is spent with small and medium enterprises.[33] It is not parochial, narrow minded, or inappropriate to suggest universities should squeeze every penny into procurement with social value in whatever economic situation certain regions find themselves in. The way out of this economic crash can be led by business, but universities can also flex their muscles to contribute significantly to that recovery. This should include commissioning where there are returns aligned to growing local employment, building requirements into contracts around local investment, and supporting local business wherever that opportunity exists. This model will support a recovery, and it will also help future recoveries, placing universities at the heart of an ecosystem of local supply, anchored to the place they are based, supporting the viability of local businesses who can recruit graduates, using their position to achieve social good. This also helps with that persistent problem of who *feels* the benefit. Universities should turn every transaction into an opportunity to showcase their work. Every purchase should support the growth of the best people doing the best work in local industries and communities. In the wider economic climate, value remains crucial, but this is about a shared financial burden, and a recognition that through their sheer scale universities can leverage long-term financial benefits for impactful good.

The foundations of universities are solid and with global appeal. They have relatively stable income and an irreplaceable role in government agenda, irrespective of the party of government. In the short-term, a funding squeeze caused by COVID pressures could impact new recruitment and add to the job crisis. In response, universities should also look at how they can directly employ more graduates and not only within academic roles. In recognising their success is tied to the places they are based, universities should be the keystones in developing public sector graduate schemes. This would draw funding from wider public sector partners and give students the opportunity to work with a number of employers, and in turn mean they gain a range of experience. The public sector employers would benefit from their shared experience, and no single institution would bear the cost of their employment.

A rapid expansion of these programmes may not make a seismic difference to graduate employment but it will make a significant difference to students who take part. Coupled with the thousands of students who already work in universities and students' unions in part-time roles, a well targeted graduate scheme could add a few more advocates for the sector when it will surely need all the friends it can get.

Universities as local shapers

At its core, a civic solidarity, engaged with local business, helps to answer the question of how universities might address some of the local economic issues. However, this crisis will need more than warm words and better spending. Universities can go further and be active participants in creating business propositions which create local jobs, gives students opportunities, and tie them more closely to a sense of place. Anyone who has ever attended a graduation, alumni event, or even just stopped and spoken with students, will know of the incredible pride with which many speak of their university homes. Now these places need enthusiastic students more than ever. A brief look through social media will show students are entrepreneurial with many running businesses on the side of their main studies, so the drive to work locally and differently is there to be utilised. In conjunction with partners there is now the opportunity for mission groups and sector bodies to work with the business community to design new entrepreneurial support programmes for the moment we are now in. Imagine, new partnerships between governments, local civic stakeholders like mayors and local enterprise partnerships, working hand in glove with universities to create funded entrepreneurship schemes, targeted toward local conditions, and most importantly developed with the long-term in mind to give them time to succeed. This will not only be central to giving students greater skills, but can help remove risks from activities that one day could be central to the ongoing economic recovery.

It is not only students working in this space. Given the vast expertise of universities in specific research strengths, university spin-outs provide direct opportunities to boost graduate employment. University spin-outs include software providers SAGE from the University of Newcastle, Google grew from a partnership in Stanford, and, fittingly, Unite Students, which provides student accommodation across the country, grew from university research.[34] [35] If the science is already there, the funding is ready, business support exists, a perfect opportunity presents itself. If universities are to grow these opportunities, there is a role for government in ramping up funding for this translational work. The benefit of potential spin-outs is not only that they are directly creating jobs but they are tied to both universities and the wider economy. They can access specific business advice remote from other companies, they have a pool of resources to tap into from the university, and by their nature they are a unique asset in the places they are based. In giving them a boost, there is a route to employment for graduates and, crucially, there is a long-term basis in which to build distinctive economic strengths. This will not only help the brain-drain issue, and provide immediate graduate employment, it will also provide the basis for ongoing work experience and training. Government should provide more significant funding for programmes of this kind.

Universities as collaborators

With all of this in mind, there are three approaches to economic recovery to consider; one, an enhanced engagement in the local economy; two, greater mobilisation of resource to support employment, and; three, more effective business support. The final question is who gets to decide how this approach works in practise.

Universities influence their places but are less often influenced by it. Experts attend local forums, get-togethers, and civic groups. These are vital and shape the work of our places. Groups like Local Enterprise Partnerships would be much poorer were it not for the work of universities in brokering partnerships with industry and giving advice on research and development activities. However, there is not yet enough opportunity for external bodies to shape the work of universities. Councils, which act like Trustee Boards, usually have a representation from civic partners but this is too strategic to drive the work of universities on a day-to-day basis. As the University of Lincoln[36] has proposed via their

21st Century Lab initiative, universities need to be more permeable. That is, universities need to be more open to change from partners and in turn using this relationship to change their places. The 21st Century Lab manifesto presents a series of 10 interrelated grand challenges, not intended to be predictive of what will come, but instead illustrate the complex and unpredictable nature of change we are experiencing, and how universities can shape, engage, understand and educate in relation to such challenges, as a starting point. In the context of COVID, the changing needs of the labour markets are unpredictable and fast moving, so having employers, civic partners, and others central to shaping curriculum, career offers, and the approach to creating demand for graduates will be necessary. This gives partners a genuine stake in the future of the organisation. Crucially, it also ties the success of universities to their local area, not just the success of their local area to universities.

This is a long-term ambition but there will be immediate crises in the interim. If universities can employ better, buy better, build better, and share better, then they can support existing local industry better. It is inevitable that some jobs and industries will not fully recover from COVID-19, but the extent of the damage is within the sector's collective gift. If there is an asynchronous recovery between universities and their places, universities could pay their students directly to gain work experience in local businesses. In particular, targeting SMEs (small to medium enterprises) and specific sectors in high growth will achieve a social and economic good. This can be joined to funded projects and short-term opportunities for students and graduates to work with hard-hit sectors who need immediate access to skills and resources for a quick recovery, which would include industries such as tourism and leisure, and would in turn support the viability of businesses in the short term, grow already viable businesses, and give a boost to the whole ecosystem.

The future of the economy is uncertain but that does not mean universities are powerless. The new university calls on higher education to not only be a provider of great skills but to unlock their potential as a shaper of economies, a supporter of business, a booster of students, and a reliable, compassionate, and accessible partner, reaching the people, places, and businesses deemed unreachable by others, and doing well by doing the right thing.

Chapter 2:
The Crisis of Opportunity

Why should you care?

We all have a stake in our universities. Even if neither you nor anybody you know has ever stepped onto a campus, you have probably contributed to your local university. This is because universities are a public service funded by the public purse and their activity plays an enormous role in our social and economic wellbeing.

The funding of higher education is therefore of central concern to our whole society. This concern has only become more acute after the 2008 financial crash. Tuition fees for undergraduate programmes are a relatively recent phenomenon. In 1998 the then Labour Government introduced fees of £1,000 per year of higher study, topping these up in 2006 to £3,000. In 2012, the

Conservative-Liberal democratic government ushered in fees of £9,000, and after subsequent small adjustments they today stand at £9,250. It was believed that in introducing a high ceiling for fees, providers would charge variable rates and encourage competition. Of course, what happened was that all providers rushed to the fee cap, and today no real discounting based on fees exists for home undergraduate students. Universities do use part of their income to offer students bursaries based on their household income, though there is little evidence these are an effective market mechanism which supports student decision making or encourages competition.[1]

This isn't the case for postgraduate students who are often funded by a mix of government loans, research grants, and self-funding. Equally, international students are usually self-funded, and pay significantly more than their UK counterparts. For example, an undergraduate international student studying at LSE in 2021 would pay £22,430 per year of study compared to a maximum of £9,250 with their peers from the UK.[2] In Scotland, tuition is generally free for Scottish students. In Wales, fees are capped at £9,000, while in Northern Ireland they are capped at £4,395 for students from Northern Ireland and the Republic of Ireland.

Basically, this means that universities receive a lot of cash every year. For students studying under the current system in England, the £9,250 is mostly sent straight from government to universities. This is repaid once a student earns just over £27,000 at a rate of 9% of their earnings above this amount. This is written off after 30 years or when the balance is cleared. This system means that the vast majority of student loans are never paid off and over half of the forecast cost of loans (currently £17.6 billion) in higher education is written off.[3] This may not appear on pay cheques, council tax letters, or invoices, but nonetheless it is a real debt which drives government spending decisions.

People should care about this because if a government believes that controlling public spending is important, it can only control the bill for higher education in a few ways. Either it limits the number of people who can go to university (this could be you, or someone you care about), it reduces funding to universities (your local one could shut or teach fewer programmes), it makes university more expensive to individuals, or it socialises the debt through increased taxation or more generous repayment terms. The government has attempted to sell this debt but a mix of economics and accounting make this unviable.[4] Perhaps even more damaging, increasing numbers of programmes cost more to teach than the current tuition fee levels can cover.[5] Inflation worsens this problem over time, and in the post-COVID-19 world, there is no guarantee UK universities will continue to recruit international students in such high numbers, though at time of writing, data from UCAS applications and sector studies suggest ongoing growth in applications from non-EU countries remains close to pre-pandemic rates if not slightly exceeding them.[6 7]

Asking people to believe in the value of a whole sector on the basis that it is a social good is a stiff challenge. You might argue that government should instead fund universities from general taxation, so that everybody would feel like they have a stake. Or that students should pay for it themselves, so that only people who were really motivated would go. Or that you want a middle ground, where government only funds the programmes which will pay for themselves through high wages. These approaches do not address the question of how individuals might feel more connected to their local institutions, and in turn raises other issues of exclusivity and access. The funding of higher education is a collective obligation with some very obvious beneficiaries, but not everyone has a direct stake in it at present.

The way higher education is funded is therefore about the collective decisions society makes about what we value. If the future is going to need *more* skilled workers, then one way to develop a shared, prosperous, and equal society with a connection to its publicly-funded universities is expanding the opportunity to attend. This argument is seldom made in the news or by politicians of any party. It is perfectly reasonable to make the argument that not every student financially benefits from going to university.[8] However, picking the subjects and universities students can attend requires a level of foresight into the future of the economy no person, business, or government can divine. In any case, the loss of opportunity to attend university would not only be a loss for individuals but a loss for the places who benefit from well-funded universities, the influx of students, and the retention of skilled graduates. The benefits universities bring to society, students, skills and local economies, means the United Kingdom needs a larger, higher education sector, not a smaller one.

Who gets in?

The opportunity to attend university depends on many factors, including a student's qualifications, how much their family earns, whether their parents went to university, and their social demographics. If higher education is to be the great social leveller that so many hope it to be (and the sector promises it to be), then part of that promise has to be that those who would most benefit from it can most easily access it.

Although the growth of the university sector has been uneven, the idea that more education is a good thing has been, historically, a relatively mainstream political position. To take even a recent timeline, there was the expansion of universities in the Robbins Report,[9] originally published in 1963, underpinning many of the changes to the British higher education since, and the conversion of former colleges to universities in the Further and Higher Education Act 1992.[10] Coupled with an increase in the funding for higher education in enacting the Dearing Report, and Browne Review,[11] there is a sector which has been continually getting bigger, in turn allowing more people to attain the promise of a university education. In recent history the number of applicants accepted through UCAS rose from 271,000 in 1994 to 570,000 in 2020.[12] Importantly for access, entrance for part-time programmes has declined by more than 50% since 2008/9 owing to changes in funding, regulation, and programme provision.[13]

As of 2019/20 there were just over 2.5 million people studying in higher education. This is 600,000 more than were studying in 2000/2001.[14] In that period there has been more than an additional 230,000 post-graduate students. The increase varies by provider but it does not seem that universities have yet satisfied the collective appetite for more education. Indeed, despite the occasional panic that increasing fees, online study, Massive Open Online Courses, international alterna-tives, private providers, or COVID-19 would break universities, the sector has been continually and histor-ically robust. Despite the gloom that often descends on the sector, the continual growth of international student numbers, the relative financial success, and the genuinely world-leading education and research strengths, makes higher education one of the UK's most competitive and enviable assets.[15]

Growing opportunities for students, and not just absolute student numbers, is a key part of maintaining social mobility after the pandemic. The inequalities which exist on entry to university follow a student through to the degree classifications they receive, and the jobs they get on graduation. The disadvantages faced by those who lack financial power, who have been denied opportunity because of their race, gender, or disability, or who simply do not have the affects of a middle or upper class upbringing, do not disappear when a student enters university. Nor do they disappear when they leave higher education. There is an intersection between class, race, gender, and disability, which can be discerned from the university regulators data. It demonstrates a complex picture of varying access, continuation, progression and attainment, by different demographics. However, understanding this is the case does not bring an ever more equal university closer. Society has multiple dimensions of inequalities, and universities are part of society, reflecting back many of the structural issues and barriers people face. This, however, should not be a reason for resigned inaction, but a spur to set an example for society more generally. The inequities are longstanding but in a period of disrupted education, arrested household incomes, and long-term economic scarring, closing these gaps becomes even more urgent.

The proportion of 18-year-olds securing a place at university with UCAS rose to 37% in 2020.[16] As of 2019, under 20% of state-funded students progress on to the universities with the highest entry grades; only 13% of looked-after children progress to higher education by age 19, and just over 26% of students who have free school meals at age 15 enter higher education by age 19.[17] These are only some of the axis through which progress into higher education can be measured. In the thirteen years between 2007 and 2020, white pupils had the lowest percentage entry rate into college or university of all state school students.[18] However, the percentage gap difference between white and Black students getting a 1st or 2:1 stands at 20%. This is a significant reduction from a 26.3% gap in 2014 but still a shockingly large chasm to bridge.[19] It is also the case that white students are the most likely of all ethnic groups to be in sustained employment or study one year after graduation.[20] There is also a strong correlation between levels of disadvantage on entering higher education and earnings on graduation.[21] There is some headway in a number of these areas institutionally, but not enough to close yawning inequality gaps any time soon. The progress in entry for students from Black, Asian and minority ethnic backgrounds shows that while more needs to be done, gaps need not be permanent, immutable, nor cannot be tackled. To do so will require a concerted effort by those able to action significant change, and clarity on the issue that is being tackled. The statistics here paint a clear picture that closing educational inequalities is complex but it is not impossible. Higher education can be a social good and this is why so many people want to access it, this is why it is funded ultimately through taxation, and this is why we should always strive for it to deliver ever more benefit for more people.

This is a particularly urgent concern while facing a future where economic shocks could impact government funding, university capacity, and individual aspiration. Universities are an effective temporary buffer that provide space to learn and grow while being funded, and as establishments they attract a wage premium even if that premium is uneven.[22] If this ecosystem is damaged it will be bad for the sector, bad for individuals, and bad for society. It will be particularly bad for those working class children whose education is genuinely the opportunity to change their lives. The children who are first in the family to get a university place will have a future of possibilities closed to them. And, the aspirant doctors, teachers, professors, vets, and professionals who need a degree to get in the door would be cruelly locked out if education does not expand to keep up with the demand for it. The issue of entry into university is therefore ultimately shaped by perceptions of value, attainment, public spending and overcoming multifaceted systemic biases.

COVID-19 and higher education

The COVID-19 pandemic caused serious turbulence in university admissions. For a generation of teenagers, COVID meant disrupted A Levels and other qualifications, being in and out of school as governmental guidance changed, and much uncertainty about their future. What is certain is the impacts of the pandemic that run visibly down socio-economic lines. There has been a gulf in experience for those with access to technology at home, parents who can support their learning, and a safe learning environment, compared to those for whom being away from school, and placed into a difficult situation at home, meant a loss of an important support structures, a hot meal, and place of safety.[23]

Despite these difficulties, 2020, the year of the first COVID cohort, was a strong year for university admissions. Largely because of the award of centre-assessed grades, grades allocated by teachers not exams, algorithms or exam boards, pupils did better than ever. There were 570,475 applicants, up by 29,200 compared to 2019; a record number of acceptances; and a near 10% increase in places for students aged 25-29.[24] This methodology also had positive impacts in widening access to higher education. Record numbers of students from the lowest participation neighbourhoods entered higher education, more students from the poorest backgrounds entered the universities with the highest entry grades, and a record number of students declaring a disability entered higher education.[25] This demonstrates two important facts. The first is that dramatic progress in access to higher education at times requires blunt instruments. If exams present a distinct barrier to improving the social mobility of thousands of young people then it's necessary to consider the nature, grading, and prominence of exams. The second, is that there are policy levers available to radically improve access. The question is how to balance equality of assessment with the inequality in results it breeds.

Allocating grades based on teacher assessment has not solved all educational inequalities, however, it is encouraging that there is little evidence that grade allocations showed systematic biases.[26] It has turned out (so far) that teachers can make reasonable assessments of students' performance and universities could accept applicants in greater numbers, all while the sector did not crumble when confronted with new ways of operating. It should also be said that the ability for universities to respond to a whole new set of admissions criteria in next to no time shows that they can be nimble, responsive, and accommodating, even at their most pressured time of year – if they choose to be.

The challenge now is how to take the best of this energy and approach into the future. There will come a time when government will choose to return to grading, assessment, and a more traditional application process of some kind. The efforts of the whole education sector should now be turned toward ensuring the progress made in access is not reversed. This means ensuring that the future students applying to university without centre assessed grades but with significant lost learning are given as much opportunity as possible to demonstrate their suitability for a degree programme. For universities, this means not only a more flexible admissions process in the treatment of grades, interviews, and auditions, but a clear analysis of how their teaching should account for this learning loss. The enormity of this challenge calls for the whole education sector to work together to prevent a generation of young people having a poor learning, admissions, and university teaching, experience.

So what?
More students deserve the opportunity of going to university to accrue its many benefits. To make this an achievable reality, the sector has to make a strong case for more governmental support. A crisis such as the one we currently face does not call for a smaller university

sector; that feels like a reckless risk to assume the nation's economic future is best served by this when there's much potential on what university can offer. The unmovable facts at present are that the workforce of the future is increasingly geared towards more education, not less; the movable part is where universities can develop this beyond the mechanics of sending more people out into the world with degrees.

Even in a record year of applications in the midst of a pandemic, there were still over 150,000 applicants (22% of the total) who were not placed in a university through UCAS.[27] This is before considering the number of people over 18 who feel they are too old to study, that university is too much of a risk, or that they can't fit the workload amongst other commitments. Most people are living longer and will work in industries that require continual changes, and yet they are barred from further education by student finance rules which mean you usually cannot receive funding to study a second degree level qualification. This is before considering the immense social value of having a period of stability to learn and grow, and to be funded to do so.

The goal should be more education. If universities are to live up to their social promise of improving the lives of the people they teach and the fortunes of the places they are based, the only way they can defend their value, support their local communities, and make a real difference to educational attainment, is to both increase the volume of students and enhance the diversity of their intake. It is admittedly a huge undertaking, one that relies on a more robust and supportive structure for both staff and students alike, but it's an ambition worth aiming for. There will always be barriers to entry, and obstacles in facilitating larger-scale change; if higher education is one of our great success stories, then everyone should have the opportunity to be a beneficiary of it.

There is enough debate on higher education admissions reform to fill several lengthy tomes; never mind a short book such as this. However, there is pressing need to consider what facilitates more people getting in and getting on across undergraduate and postgraduate study, in a way that is achievable, accessible and – crucially – truly valuable.

Getting in

There is an expectation, or an illusion perhaps, that university success relies solely on high performance through school, putting pressure to think about the future on increasingly lower ages to achieve grades, and projecting a sense of failure on many who do not. This is not the case. Nearly 40% of 19-year-olds do not have A Level or equivalent qualifications, but this does not have to mean they cannot achieve university degrees.[28] Foundation years provide students with the opportunity to study subjects, usually at a university, which allow them to progress on to pursue a full degree. Entrants to these types of programme nearly trebled between 2012-2018.[29] For students without level 3 qualifications (like A levels), they provide a genuine opportunity to change careers, access student finance, and take up new study – it also allows people of different ages and life stages to do so. In the context of the uncertainty around COVID where demand for some industries may not return, their popularity will likely grow. It is however disappointing that instead of the government welcoming this form of more flexible provision for development and career change, the most recent review of higher education instead cast doubt on their effectiveness.

The 2019 *Independent panel report to the Review of Post-18 Education and Funding*, most often called the Augar Review, found that:

'It is hard not to conclude that universities are using foundation years to create four-year degrees in order to entice students who do not otherwise meet their standard entry criteria. Most recruiters to these programmes are medium or lower entry tariff institutions, typically universities with a high proportion of students from poorer backgrounds. These students are obliged to take out an additional fourth year of higher and non-cancellable fee loans. We question whether this is in their best interests.'[30]

Nobody can blame the authors of the Augar Review for not anticipating COVID-19, but it's worth pausing on the sentiment within this statement. There isn't strong evidence that students regret taking foundation years – they provide effective entry into study for older learners,[31] and they are facilitated by a wide range of providers (Oxford perhaps being the most atypical in this narrative).[32] One of the motivations of the marketisation of higher education was to enhance student choice. For the panel to divine student interest based on household income ignores both the access benefit of foundation years to students with lower household incomes[33] and the differences in attainment for poorer children.[34] Work by LSE most compellingly demonstrates that there is a direct line between an adult's socio-economic class and their child's GCSE results.[35] If there is significant evidence that foundation years are being used to exploit students then that should call for stronger regulation, not their removal for students who benefit from them.

It doesn't have to be the case that these programmes solely benefit universities. The University of Liverpool, which offers foundation year programmes in conjunction with a local college, demonstrates their value. Unusually, the university provides these programmes in Medicine, Dentistry, and Veterinary Sciences, which generally have both high entry tariffs and less success in attracting students from working class backgrounds. Students have called these programmes life-changing. Even better, this first year is cheaper than a usual level of undergraduate fees, and provides students to the college that teaches it. In terms of government objectives, the opportunity provides pathways into highly skilled employment and a boost to the further education sector, but it also enhances social mobility and can contribute significantly to the workforce in industries or vocations where more people are needed. It is a win for all the parties involved.

Rather than questioning their value, the government should prioritise the expansion of foundation years of this kind. They provide routes into highly skilled employment, they can support the growth of the further education sector, and they allow students without traditional qualifications to get into higher education. Responsibility for encouraging their growth sits with government, providers, and the long-term beneficiaries of these programmes – employers. In the post COVID-19 landscape it would be beneficial for everyone to have more opportunities to change career, and dismissing these courses' value in favour of a standardised, singular exclusive route is to ignore their vital contributions to both individuals, and society more broadly.

Even with access programmes, and despite the availability of student loans, leaving full-time employment in order to study in any form is a risk. It's not just that there is a learning gap to bridge, but that it fundamentally changes people's lives and careers. To de-risk this transition there needs to be options to study foundation years in alternative ways. Not everyone can access programmes between 9am and 5pm, especially if they have caring responsibilities, work, or the various commitments that crop up in the fullness of life. Our world is increasingly less glued to the 9-to-5 structure and this movement will place pressure on universities too. Universities should seek to provide these foundation years outside of the traditional classroom experience, and teach at the time available to these students. This would typically involve evenings, weekends, and through online means where appropriate. It needs to be as easy as possible for students to transition into new modes of learning, building towards qualification. This is likely to come at an additional cost in infrastructure, but this could be offset if it were possible to grow the total number of students – the quality of this new infrastructure for those students would generate positive feedback and tangible results, in turn attracting more to education, and on the cycle goes. Government, as part of their lifetime skills guarantee, should ensure student loan rules are sufficiently flexible for this cohort.

Even with additional flexibility, it might be difficult for students to pick up these programmes alongside full-time employment, particularly if they have been away from education for a long time. This is, again, where government can step in. The government should provide financial incentives for employers to release their employees for days, or short periods of time, to undertake foundation year programmes. If the government is worried about the rapid growth of the university sector this could be where there is the most strategic alignment with local employer's needs. This means that employers would be encouraged to release their students and would develop a more direct relationship to the type of education they are receiving. In turn, the growing number of students studying flexibly in foundation years would apply upward pressure to universities to provide more flexible options in part-time and online study, which is another important way to increase the accessibility of higher education.

In return for this growing ecosystem we should also expect universities to support the wider viability of the further education sector. Delivering foundation years within further education colleges promises some distinct benefits which might not be achievable in a higher education setting. There is, firstly, a familiarity benefit in that students could be placed somewhere within, or near to, their local communities. The second benefit is that it would allow for both cost-sharing and new opportunities to increase the economic viability of colleges themselves. Thirdly, it would promise a new opportunity of cross-fertilisation on ideas about pedagogy and curriculum within both the further and higher education setting. This is not only crucial in supporting transitions to higher education, but also in supporting a more joined up education sector – vital if students are going to take more qualifications over their lifetime.

Going through

These measures could increase the numbers of students accessing higher education through supplying alternative entry routes. This does not address the issues around the more direct entry routes into higher education set out earlier. This is not a book about level three qualification reform, but clearly the prizing of A Levels or equivalent presents distinct barriers to entry, and sets them in place from an early age. Fundamentally, entry into university depends on the extent to which they are valued; and the extent to which their shortcoming in reflecting a whole student experience can be mitigated.

COVID-19 has shown that teachers can make reasonable assessments of a student's performance. For many, that was never in doubt. Students are not dropping out in huge numbers,[36] and the allocation of grades, rather than the award through testing, has been good for closing gaps in disparities in entry. Clearly, teachers do not want to set their students up to fail, and they want to award opportunities fairly across a cohort, and not just individually. No single measure is perfect. Predicted grades are fraught with the dangers of biases and data suggests that on average most student cohorts are over-predicted their grades.[37] Equally, in light of the removal of AS levels, teachers are partially making these judgements based on ongoing learning and GCSE results, which are also problematic predictors of future performance.[38] But it is also true that though A levels, in theory, reward effort, they are liable to students having a bad day, bad questions, or just bad luck, in their capacity to answer the question.

Despite the primacy of A levels as a supposed equal chance for attainment, universities already consider a range of factors on entry like which school a student attended or the higher education participation rates of their area. As the Director of Fair Access and Participation at university regulator the Office for Students stated, 'A level grades can only be considered to be a robust measure of potential if they are considered alongside the context in which they are achieved.'[39] One of the lessons of the pandemic is that A levels are an important piece of information for university admissions but they do not have to be the sole one. This period will be defined by the disruption to education.

One reform, of benefit to all students, is not only to make it clear that a range of factors will be considered, thereby encouraging a wider range of applicants, but providing a wider range of opportunities to prove their talents. If universities are ever going to rapidly expand proven measures like contextual offers, access pathways, and funding for under-represented groups, now is the time to do it. Taking a leaf from the book of employers, this could include a guaranteed additional assessment opportunity for under-represented groups within institutions who attain a minimum grade threshold. This should not be so cumbersome as to discourage additional applicants, but a genuine second opportunity for students disadvantaged by the current system. This disadvantage will only be exacerbated by COVID-19 and filter through for years where students have had their learning interrupted; it is key that universities tackle it head on before it can worsen.

Equally, universities already run extended outreach schemes, which include reduced offers, pathways, and financial support (which they are obliged to do), to support students into higher education. This will undoubtedly continue to be of crucial importance, but sometimes blunter tools are necessary to overcome significant systematic underrepresentation. Ring-fencing a proportion of university places for cohorts who are under-represented within a provider would lead to a more level playing field. Universities like St Andrews are nudging closer to such a system where they guarantee an offer for students who meet a lower minimum entry grade, are care experienced, and/or are from the 20% most deprived areas of Scotland and attend a school which has 30% or lower progression to higher education.[40] The likes of Imperial College London[41] and the University of Glasgow[42] offer variations on guaranteed offers if a student whose background means they are less likely to attend manages to meet minimum criteria. This is good but across the UK gaps in entry are still large. A more progressive system would see universities allocate a priority of places for under-represented demographics within their institutions. This should guarantee that the students facing the largest barriers, the same cohorts most vulnerable to profound economic shocks such as the one we are facing, would have a more level playing field. This means applicants would have greater confidence in the system, more students would be able to get into higher tariff providers, and in a system where higher education is expanded overall, no student need miss out on a place. This would need more robust regulation by the Office for Students, but given regulation on these targets already exists this would not be a wholly new system, but one that could be developed upon existing infrastructure.

This should not be delivered as a dispassionate exercise on a spreadsheet. For universities this should include programmes which are based in, run from, and employ staff in, the parts of their local area which have lower access to higher education. If university success is about a cultural, social, and economic fit, every piece of promotion, idea, interaction, and advocacy, should be cut in such a way that prospective students can recognise themselves in it. This is not only important for recruitment but, in an age of such uncertainty, as a beacon of hope that universities can support all students to succeed.

Success

Alongside intentional steps to improve access, it is also the case that economic crises tend to lead to more people applying to university, not fewer.[43] This does not mean these students will not still face profound financial difficulties once they get a place at university because of external changing circumstances at home or because of a decline in part-time work in student industries across the country, like bars, hotels, and restaurants. Nationally, universities are spending hundreds of millions of pounds on bursaries (financial grants awarded to students to support their ability to afford higher education), but there is mixed evidence showing that they impact student success. At the University of Bristol, bursaries were found to be ineffective recruitment tools but they were found to support students in their abilities to manage their money.[44] In Cambridge, bursary provision supported students wellbeing and allowed them to focus more on their studies.[45] A review carried out by Kings College London in 2019 suggested bursaries in some institutions had a positive outcome on degrees, and gave students peace of mind while they studied.[46] Bursaries are usually contingent on family income therefore a drop of household income due to COVID job losses or cuts in hours could mean more students receive bursaries, and given pressures on university finances, there is an imperative to spend them wisely. Universities also need to consider the relationships that bursaries can build between universities and their students, the packages of more personal support they can wrap around bursary provision, and how they position, and communicate why a student is receiving a bursary, and the benefits it can bring to both the student and the university – and in creating a feeling of community.

Money via bursaries does not solely lie at the root of all happiness for students. Student success is complex and defined differently by each student. It encompasses academic success, personal wellbeing, and getting a great job at the end of it all. This is encapsulated in the way universities structure their support, and, in the pandemic, provide a sense of optimism that things can get better during these pivotal times. When universities think about student bursaries they should always remember that they are not providing dispassionate benefits. Every payment should be used as an opportunity talk about the opportunities of university life outside of their curriculum to support that sense of belonging. Equally, every student should have the opportunity to defer their bursary payment into institutional goods, society memberships, housing discounts, bus passes, and all of those in between opportunities that build a sense of identity – a strong focus of higher education is, naturally, the education; anything that attracts or supports students should offer the fuller picture of richness and exploration available within these institutions. Finally, given the pressure universities will be facing as the country emerges from COVID, and as safeguards like allocated grades slip away, universities, regulators, and governments should place a relentless focus on student retention as a key metric of success. No student who does not need to drop out should slip through the cracks.

Flexibility

Universities can be a place of true and tangible opportunity through increasing the numbers of students getting into higher education, enhancing the representation of those students, and supporting their success through enhanced pastoral and financial support. The global crisis brought about by COVID-19 demands that universities set an example of how it is possible to get on, and do well. This can only be made feasible with a more flexible higher education provision.

The UK government has attempted to map this out in recent proposals where they imagine students can step in and out of education, taking their qualifications with them, and access student finance for the lifetime of their studies. This would be a progressive first step and could meet what will be the need for retraining and reskilling as our economy changes. However, this doesn't set out how universities, and employers, could accommodate a change on this scale in any actionable detail. This should be an urgent part of the roadmap.

It's likely that there will be significant demand for postgraduate programmes. One reform that universities could undertake is to allow undergraduate students to defer a portion of their bursary payments to their final year, matched by a university bonus, to pay for post-graduate study. This would mean that universities would have greater confidence over student numbers, students would have money to put toward their education, and the cost of the system overall could be reduced. This initiative would also give a direct incentive for students to continue their education. It could be a profound social leveller. This model would work for students who want to continue into postgraduate study – though it leaves out those returning to study, whose needs call for further thought. There has been little work into standardising progression, support, and access routes, into post-graduate study for those who do not hold undergraduate degrees. If governments were ever to show mass support for postgraduate learning an enormous information campaign on its benefits would be welcomed by the sector, students, and in the long-run, society.

Higher education institutions have necessarily shifted to online teaching over the course of the pandemic. Through this they have learnt lessons on delivery, curriculum, and keeping a student body engaged – whether through the successful implementation of this shift, or through missteps and notable discrepancies that they can learn from and improve. Online teaching is not only an option for more flexible teaching but a means through which universities can reach a truly global audience. The flexibility imagined by government falls down if they constrain their imagination to in-person delivery. The lesson from lockdown should not only be that online learning is possible but that for some students it will be preferable, even the best option. It will allow greater asynchronous content reaching those who can't study 9-to-5. It enables providers to teach through different modes appropriate to their programmes. And, crucially, it removes the need for ever more loca-tion-locked physical infrastructure, meaning that they can be scaled up more easily. Flexibility is partly about the way higher education is funded, but it is also about teaching methods and how this filters through every level. This would also make it more viable for large numbers of higher education providers to offer a number of part-time programmes, and broaden their opportunities in this realm.

This should also be the era in which university Continuing Education Departments come into their own. Continuing Education Departments within universities offer a range of programmes, for current and non-students, to study subjects and qualifications of their choosing. These have often been based on interests or taster sessions, and will absolutely have a place in the post-COVID world. In bringing in the flexibility required for this, there is a world of possibility – a new university approach would allow Continuing Education Departments to act as a hub for getting people into university. They can be genuine signposts within local communities which point toward qualifications from GCSE through to PhD, where, with additional professional partners, they could support students to get the qualifications they need for their desired path. These courses could be a true bastion of retraining and second chances, something often forgotten or secondary to the often high-school-leaver-focus within education discourse. In a world which will require ever more retraining, they could be the place that offers those tasters at a much bigger scale to help people and employers work out just what it is they should, want, and can do. Decisions on education can shape someone's life; creating as much opportunity for people to explore this before committing is vital. As provision around career advice has retreated from many of our local communities, they can genuinely be the place that acts as an anchor for all next steps.

Getting in, getting on, getting work

We previously discussed how universities can stimulate economic activity to support their places and their students. Here we have turned to addressing how opportunity can be further expanded in a post-COVID world. In some ways the solutions are simple: get more students into higher education in a way which allows greater access for those with the most need; provide the financial support, learning, time, and incentives which make this possible; bolster students and their multi-faceted needs, wants, and circumstances to have the best chance of success.

This also highlights a key debate: what is the new university for?

The pursuit of knowledge? Making the world better? Pushing the boundaries of research? Yes, to all, in theory. But it is how these proposals work together that is crucial. The purpose of the new university should be to provide the broadest possible platform to give people the skills, tools, and experiences, to change their lives.

This means a bigger sector, it means a sector which actively recruits more broadly and puts their energy into doing so, and it means a sector which gives people a second opportunity to study in a way that works for them. It means creating an infrastructure of flexibility, openness, and genuine support, so that anyone who wants to learn – no matter their circumstance – can.

Chapter 3:
The Crisis of Place

COVID-19 has brought the importance of community into sharp focus. On the one hand it's delivering food to those unable to leave their houses at the other end of the city, it's helping out neighbours in need, it's clapping on doorsteps in support of NHS workers on a cold, wet Thursday. On the other it's the shared fear of COVID hotspots, of community transmission, and of local lock-downs. At a minimum, it is a shared sense of collective obligation we have to act responsibly as to not infect one another with a dangerous virus. The reason we get frustrated with politicians, celebrities, and neighbours flouting the rules is not only because of the danger they risk but because it breaks the invisible compacts we hold with one another. If you watched the television in the days after former Secretary of State for Health Matt Hancock or Boris Johnson's Chief Adviser Dominic Cummings resigned, after their own respective flouting of the rules surrounding travel and distancing, nearly every station would ask viewers and guests if this meant they were now more likely to break the rules.

It's a strange question to consider. The popular narrative is that with the growth of mass consumer capitalism, people are becoming more individualistic. This would presumably mean people are less likely to help one another and care about the behaviour of others and students are no strangers to this prejudice. If you've ever watched programmes like *Fresh Meat* or *The Young Ones*, this caricature seems especially true of students as a mix of rebellious, feckless, funny, and primarily out to have a good time regardless of anyone else. Students *are* part of their local communities but their financial relationships to it, their more transient nature (often due to travelling between their university address and their family home), and their equally pronounced, specific university community within the wider community (these can be one in the same) make them slightly separate to it. The thousands and thousands of hours they spend volunteering and being good members of their community doesn't make for as good television, unfortunately.

It raises a cultural question of the extent to which universities are similar to the places they are based. If you visit the websites of University of the Arts London, Liverpool John Moores University, University of Stirling, and lots of others, you will find a variation on a 'COVID-19 community pledge'. On these pages universities set out how students can prevent their peers and their local communities from getting COVID. They emphasise the collective responsibility for hand washing, the social contract between universities and their communities, and potential admonishments for falling short of these standards.

This is clearly sensible advice for students but it is also savvy public relations from universities themselves. It sends a signal to their local community that not only are their students part of it, but they are willing to enter a pseudo-contractual relationship to protect it. The extent to which this plays out in reality depends who you ask but there is little evidence that students are more irresponsible with COVID-19 than the population at large. It is interesting to think of the public concern toward students breaking rules compared to the fact that an estimated 41% of over 80s broke local lockdown rules after their first vaccine.[1]

This is about universities projecting an image out into their communities, one which seeks to reassure and also says that the university will act as a guardian of last resort. In some ways, it might always be inevitable that universities feel a bit different to the places they are based so use measures like this to emphasise their similarities. After all, they are often amongst the wealthiest institutions in towns and cities with their own campuses and facilities available largely for the people who pay to be there. Culturally, they enjoy less contact with the public at large than the local hospital and their assets, like teaching and research, are available to few people outside of the university itself.

Why everyone wants a university except the people who don't

If only everyone was as optimistic about universities as those who visit and work with them! Speak to any university staff member and you will find that some of their best memories are from the conversations with the parents of children who want to attend their university; with the children who turn up for a visit open-mouthed at this wonderful institution on their doorstep they had never seen; and from providing the unmatchable joy in making promised educational experiences come true. Universities make an indelible mark on those who visit them. Their names can be evocative of the places, people, histories, and regions in which they are deeply rooted. If universities have a role, a new role, in shaping our places then their task is to bring more people from the outside in, and they should be doing the work taking the place on the inside to those out.

Places like Oxford or Cambridge are synonymous of the universities which occupy them. Campus-based universities can have a significant impact on the location in which they sit; it's unsurprising that a number of areas would actively support one in their own community – Ben Everitt MP, for example, noted his support for a brand new university for Milton Keynes, deeming it 'so vital for our future economy'.[2] For anyone who has lived in cities like Manchester, Leeds, Edinburgh, Liverpool, or Sheffield, the place just *feels* different when students have gone home for the summer. This is a question of economics and regeneration but it's also something harder to grasp. A university confers a status, a vibrancy, a cultural signifier, indicating the place has activity that people want to share in. They shape a place like few institutions can. Take the North East of England, for example. Teesside University campus in Darlington provides community sports and childcare so learners can come together and keep learning. The enormous investment into Northumbria and Newcastle universities forms a key part of the architectural design of the city.

There are of course accounts of students being disruptive, noisy, and drinking too much in the local community, and there are serious, legitimate concerns about the disruption of local housing markets by housing developments geared toward students. Houses of multiple occupancy can lead to 'student areas', which in some instances have changed the nature of local communities. In most major cities you will hear conversations about the volume of student accommodation being built over other services and across increasingly widening communities. The richness of the cultural influences students and their universities bring has to be balanced with the knowledge that this isn't felt by everybody. It is of no use telling families whose neighbours have sold their property to developers that their university has some interesting galleries and museums. It is inadequate to limit the response to concerns around how people feel about their places to economic arguments relating to universities and their cities. It is condescending for the sector to tell the families whose children are only more unlikely to attend universities, or indeed may have no interest in attending, that their local university is in fact a very good thing, and expect no one to question it. Universities must show their places that they are on their communities' side, and not just tell them that they are. Universities need to listen. COVID-19 has shown that they can, if they so choose. In times of emergency, universities have made symbolic but also crucially effective community interventions. Their students have graduated early to work in hospitals. The noisy neighbours are volunteer vaccinators. Car parks have been turned over to the NHS. Bikes have been borrowed, PPE produced, and experts have engaged in issues from the 'Test and Trace' system to finding a suitable road to recovery at pace. Universities deliver benefits to the people who study on their campuses, but they can also influence the quality of life for entire communities. The emergence from the pandemic should be the moment when universities show they can listen to their local communities, and act in their service going forward, not only when a national emergency demands it.

There will be some businesses who do not recover, there are voluntary organisations which have become terminally overstretched, and bonds between communities may be eroded through necessarily enforced separation and distancing. Universities can either help to hold distinct strands together, or they can conduct business as usual and risk letting those hit the hardest by the pandemic fall by the wayside. There is no in-between. There are no easy solutions to the challenges posed by the need to rebuild local economies while maintaining a distinct sense of place, without building walls around their academic communities. Just because they aren't easy, however, doesn't mean they should be cast aside.

Culture and the hidden superpowers of higher education

Our public estate is shrinking. Pubs are closing, religious observance is on the decline,[3] public space is being snatched away by private interest,[4] and our atomised working lives, fuelled by the proliferation of zero-hour contracts, are wrecking work-life balance for many.[5] It is obvious to anyone who has endured the COVID-19 pandemic that it has greatly disrupted our shared lives – not only in the closure of businesses, but in our more immediate social relationships. The in and out school year. The ability to visit family and loved ones. The lapsing of memberships, the quiet death of a regular get together, and a discomfort in seeing lots of people after seeing so few.

People can't do Zoom quizzes forever. They soon become boring, and everyone is sick of the friend who keeps winning them. Their growth was in lieu of other options, as a parable for our isolated plight. An often-free space (for a short time, if your friend has a paid subscription you can 'borrow') that anybody can visit, around areas of common interest. They are an unusual fusion of a publicly-available forum and a space that is closed to unwelcome visitors. Online engagement isn't going to rebuild our social fabric – though it can contribute to the building of communities.

The position of universities within our wider public spaces is equally muddled. They are publicly-funded institutions whose physical manifestation is shut off from the public at large. I can no more turn up to a lecture at a university I don't attend than I could visit the Groucho Club. This is an unusual dynamic, and universities tacitly acknowledge this in their provision of public lectures, freely available galleries, and the occasional sporting event. The public may see an outline of the institution, as though through frosted glass, but they cannot get close enough to work out what is really going on.

The ability to bring the cultural side of the university to an extended audience is about fairness, funding, and feeling part of a wider community. During COVID-19, universities took their hitherto hidden treasures to audiences in innovative ways. 'Culture at Home' brought the academic expertise of the University of Liverpool to children and parents to maintain education.[6] The University of Aberdeen has a virtual Egyptian tomb available to anyone with sufficient internet connection,[7] while the University of Leeds has delivered a meta-experience in an online session reflecting on how COVID-19 has impacted arts and culture.[8] Add in Plymouth and the Ancient Mariner,[9] Cumbrian students' online art exhibition,[10] Brighton's winter showcase,[11] and many other examples, and there is a burgeoning ecosystem of universities showing off their best when times have been at their worst.

This is only scratching the surface of what is possible. Universities have accumulated treasures of all descriptions. Part of their mission and their research lies in analysing these assets and in bringing them to the attention of the wider public. It is a secret superpower of our institutions that there are more than 100 university museums which hold an astonishing number of national treasures.[12] It would be a missed opportunity if in the rush to return to normality the sector lost the means of access that this online world brings to those who may not have visited universities, those without the financial means of doing so, and those whose access needs made the whole place exclusionary in the first place.

The return of the old normal

People like to see each other. For all the benefits of online connection, not being able to physically share space with other people is alienating. This is one of the reasons why lockdowns are deeply awful. Online resources are all well and good, but the cultural sector is reliant on national and international travellers, and often focused on in-person gathering. This has left it particularly vulnerable. The Organisation for Economic Co-operation and Development (OECD), for example, highlight that policy responses to supporting cultural industries through COVID-19 have often been inadequate as financial support packages have been ill-suited to the diversity of the sector and its workforce.[13] The contrast between the speed with which support could be rolled out for the largest businesses and the speed with which it was provided for freelancers and the self-employed is an indicator of both priority and complexity – the latter seeing instalments available every few months, while leaving many 'forgotten freelancers' to fend unsupported.

The digital pivot of any university's cultural artefacts and output will help with its resilience, but it would be an inadequate policy response and compound deep inequities in places if universities became strengthened cultural hubs at the expense of other cultural organisations in their areas. Culture, if it is anything, is the manifestation of beauty, knowledge, entertainment, and insight, in our public squares made possible by institutions and individuals who provide it. Fundamentally, it connects people to those individuals and their places. The challenges the cultural sector face is a challenge to the quality of life which we all enjoy.

This enjoyment should be widely available as both a point of principle and as a practical feature of the recovery. Universities are stretched, but they are largely stable. They could provide their students with a small culture bursary, though it is not for universities to decide what is or is not culture. This could be going for a meal out with friends, visiting an exhibition, watching a football match, going to a gig, or making a trip to the theatre or museum. The reason so many universities invest in student support is they believe fitting in is key to not dropping out and this is a natural extension of that work. This would not be without cost, but introducing students to an aspect of life they may not have experienced, supporting local economies, and helping people fall in love with their place and encouraging them to stay there to work and create jobs, is surely something universities are for. In order to position universities as truly part of their wider space, initiatives to allow for student exploration within their local culture holds a lot of potential in forming stronger bonds between the institution and community, on an individual level.

The flipside of this great reopening of our cultural world is a deep scepticism within our current Conservative government about the value of creative programmes. The Secretary of State for Education revelled in students moving toward STEM programmes and sought to rebalance teaching funding away from Media Studies toward Mathematics.[14] This is a regrettable view, as, on a basic numbers level, employment rates for Arts and STEM graduates are broadly similar and you may recall the previous statistic from the British Academy, Arts, Humanities and Social Sciences Graduates which said of the ten fastest growing sectors, eight employ more graduates from Arts, Humanities and Social Sciences than other disciplines.[15] The unpredictable world of work needs students with wider, not narrower skills.

All of this hits the target but it misses the point. Our national approach to culture and creativity speaks to a wider sentiment of what is valued within higher education and how it can be defended. Education, as argued throughout, should have an identifiable and defensible economic contribution, however our public lives would be much diminished, as we have surely learned throughout the pandemic, if it were not for those becoming expert in visual arts, game design, media, performance, the written word, and those hundreds of subjects that speak to the fundamental basis of our humanity. There will be a temptation for parts of the sector to support a growth in funding to the areas where they teach. There will be a silent shaking of the head with a deep regret that more can't be done to support the arts. If the sector wishes to support its place and save its own future then it needs a full-throated defence of its arts and humanities programmes. This movement needs to start now lest policy make funding them so difficult they become confined to a few well-funded universities making them an ever more exclusive pursuit, for an ever more exclusive set of people.

Creativity first

Getting people back into the world, telling the world that creative arts are worthwhile, and showcasing the best of universities' assets, is all valuable, and will help the places in which universities are based. The last corner of the square is embedding culture into wider programmes of economic renewal as to ensure the sector is so central to our lives that it can never be threatened again. Look at the economic recovery plan of your local area – most local authorities will have one tucked away on their website, if not already in the archive – and check whether they are considering the creative sectors as part of their economic recovery and whether they highlight the link between universities and the creative sector.

Consideration of these issues is inconsistent. Though not surprising, this is strange, given that the COVID-19 response has been such a distinctly creative endeavour. The response drew on advertisers and writers to change behaviours around social distancing. The art and design efforts put into the manufacture of face masks and PPE made people safer. The ability to understand and engage with communities is born from psychological, sociological and anthropological traditions. And this is before reflecting on the private sector, whose recovery is dependent on brand recognition, customer engagement, eye-catching campaigns, and using the full range of creative endeavours to capture spending habits.

It is not as easy to draw a straight line between creative work, COVID recovery, and place as it is in relation to STEM programmes. However, in imbuing places with vibrancy and economic activity, it is the role of the university sector to highlight the full range of contributions to the recovery at hand. This means that when sitting round those committees, panels, and drafting those documents on COVID-recovery, it is necessary to foreground the role of creative industries. This is partly because the post-COVID challenges are complex and require a multi-disciplinary approach. Rebuilding our places is a question of economics, psychology, civic design, investment, partnership, and the ability to develop a shared sense of optimism for the people that universities serve. This can't be done for free. If their whole electoral strategy is based on place and levelling up, with the aim of making places more appealing and prosperous, there is a clear imperative to fund research projects which align with these objectives. This can be from the aspiration of living in beautiful sustainable cities, to smaller but equally vital incremental improvements in our places.

Universities have an important opportunity to promote their own cultural work, bring people back together, and foreground cultural development in their communities as we recover from COVID-19. This will not be easy to achieve everywhere. Places come with inbuilt advantages and disadvantages, and the government will not be in a position to level up every city, town and village, but in advocating for a stronger input in the culture and the communities surrounding our institutions, the possibilities to thrive grow significantly. This will involve a mix of responses to a place: hard-edged economic investment, together with the optimism that we can and will make our places brilliant.

Chapter 4:
The Crisis of Relevance

It may be that I am overstating the importance of place. After all, with digital connectivity, the world is getting smaller. Those who are geographically apart are now closer than ever. Even universities, while hugely different in their composition, to the untrained eye may seem to teach broadly similar subjects to broadly similar age ranges.

One major advantage that universities enjoy is that they are relatively permanent. They don't go bankrupt (at least not those in the public sector, and not so far). They create reliable jobs. They attract people, companies, and investment, in broadly predictable ways. And they are good for businesses through educating a skilled work-force and working on research projects. Some research taking place in universities may be so abstract as to have little real-world impact. Some will focus exclusively on solving industrial problems. There is then a middle spot of the scientific breakthroughs which have far-reaching industrial and societal implications – for instance the discovery of graphene, which promises to advance our approach in energy storage with all the significant benefits that will come with it, isolated by researchers at the University of Manchester.

Perhaps universities don't just help distinguish a place, but are equally distinguished by their places. It is no coincidence that the University of Sheffield has distinct strengths in manufacturing, given its industrial heritage. It is not by stroke of fate that the University of Aberdeen has a myriad of programmes in oil and gas management. The quality of research is partly measured by its real-world impact. Place gives universities a broader purpose, which in turn allows them to make impact beyond the abstract.

COVID-19 has brought about a global pandemic, but its resolution is dependent on a close ecosystem of local actors. Vaccines were produced quickly because of funding from government, engagement with the private sector, and the years of patient support that lay behind this work. It has taken the talent of individuals and their research teams to turn the tide, but this was only made possible by the commitment of entire institutions. And this research will be needed again. Zoonotic diseases, those which transfer from humans to animals, are the leading cause of global pandemics.[1] In recent memory, swine flu, bird flu, and Ebola are just some of the most obvious examples.

Nurturing local ecosystems of research activity is both a safeguard and a path to economic recovery. COVID-19 will not be the only health threat humanity faces in this century. It is not even the only global threat. Climate change and its impacts continue to wreak havoc across the globe. We stand at a precipice of irreversible damage caused by rising temperatures fuelled by human activity. In the marshalling of resource, government intervention, and civic engagement, there is a lesson to be learned from the pandemic in how we tackle our most urgent challenges – again, should we choose to do so.

Choosing the tools

Understanding the nature of university research is the first step in valuing it. Universities carry out research with benefits that can be transferred to the public and private sector. It could be about process efficiencies, the discovery of new materials and new methods of working, inventions, insights, data, software, and so on. Its economic and social value attracts investment in facilities, retains a talented workforce, encourages the development of new industries, enhances existing business practices, and can improve the lives of people living in an area. For example, research into hydrogen fuel cells is not only an academic pursuit. It could allow transport companies to secure a competitive advantage, provide social benefits in greener cities, and secure green jobs in transport.

Governments the world over are keen on this arrangement. Tony Blair and Gordon Brown's Science and Innovation Framework sought to enhance government collaboration with business and universities, and David Cameron suggested that government could invest in non-marketable fundamental research while increasing market incentives for commercial work. As far back as 1963, Harold Wilson asserted that investment in innovation was not only a public good but would reshape the fundamentals of business and labour relations.[2]

The 2021 government is no different. In its latest iteration of this ambition, it has pledged to increase investment in Research and Development (R&D) to 2.4% of Gross Domestic Product (GDP). While in real-terms cash R&D expenditure has grown steadily for a number of years[3] as a proportion of GDP, it fell 0.3% between 1981 and 2018. In terms of international comparison, the UK sits below Australia and the Czech Republic, 0.3% behind the EU average, 0.7% behind the OECD average, and a huge 3.2% behind Israel as the largest investors in R&D.[4] The announcement of £22 billion of public funding in the drive to reach 2.4% of GDP spend is unusual not because of its ambition but because it is concrete.

Research spend in England is skewed toward the South East, so that even a minor rebalancing could have a large impact on place. Although universities are not the largest spender on R&D,[5] their research, collaboration, partnerships, and fundamental research make them the key enablers of the whole R&D ecosystem. Therefore, to improve their place in the context of COVID-19 they must develop an understanding of how they are going to steer this ecosystem.

The first thing the sector needs going forward is clarity on what this uplift in research spend will achieve. Yes, it is intended to make research more impactful – but to what end? There is a requirement to allocate public funding in the most *efficient* way to reach 2.4%, and in the most *effective* way to reach wider government priorities. The hazards are evident. For example, there might be an attempt to level up by devolving the whole public sector portion of the R&D spending uplift to regions, with no guarantee that would attract sufficient external investment. Or government could develop a more generous tax system, or more ambitious market mechanisms to attract private investors, and while this could bring in more investment it would probably exacerbate existing funding inequalities. For example, arguably, investing more in the place with the most financial clout could attract even more investment, but this would leave other places even further behind.

Research for impact

The university sector has four broad place-based functions in relation to its research.

The first is that universities are generally perceived as neutral brokers in the places they are based. It can articulate priorities in ways that other partners cannot. The university, or a group of universities, also often have a wider view of the full range of partners available to a given place. This is because unlike organisations within the public sector they are not wholly tied to a place and unlike the private sector their partnerships are not fuelled by profit. COVID-19 demonstrates that effective place-based research around health and life sciences, for instance, requires a mix of public and private partners, different sectors, and a huge range of actors within those sectors. In this sense, universities have the convening role of articulating a shared view of a research strategy within a region. This will enable partners to speak with one voice to funders. It allows projects to be better coordinated and be more than the sum of their parts. And it sends a signal to government and prospective partners about the distinctive strength of a place. It is a more efficient way to work.

This forms the basis for setting out the mechanisms which will achieve the research objectives. There is a strident debate on whether or not government should devolve research funding to regions so they may spend it the things most important to them. A regional approach may well be appropriate in some places, but not everywhere. It would also miss the point that ultimately the objective should be a national funding ecosystem which builds on latent regional strength, which allows local decision-makers greater influence, and rebalances investment. R&D can form the basis of rebalancing economic growth post COVID-19 and form more resilient growth in regions. Rather than only lobbying for devolution, universities and their regions should begin by focussing on what is the best mechanism and the most realistic mechanism for sustainable and impactful change.

In a more nuanced model, government could directly back nascent but specialist assets. There is a link between the growth of Business Expenditure on R&D (BERD) and Gross Domestic Household income.[6] BERD is strongest in areas where there are existing research strengths, so government might directly fund areas with specialisation but latent capacity to achieve broad economic benefit. For example, in the 2020 Spending Review Government committed funding for a Tees Valley Hydrogen Hub, combining an area with industrial growth potential with government priorities on sustainability.[7]

Secondly, government could steer the boat but leave others to row it by devolving funding and decision-making to an arm's length body. The Strength in Places initiative funded regional research collaborations based on existing strengths.[8] These include programmes as diverse as developing semiconductor clusters in Cardiff,[9] financial data reform in Edinburgh,[10] and work in Bristol and Bath on developing new media experiences, and enhancing local skills.[11]

There is then a third option of devolving powers, and funds, to make decisions locally about R&D investment. This has been most compellingly set out in report *The Missing £4 Billion* by Tom Forth and Richard Jones,[12] where they suggest government could allocate the uplift in R&D funding to the areas with the least public investment and where they could prove they had a convincing plan to spend it, in order to rebalance the economy. This might either be where there are existing governance structures like combined authorities or where new governance structures can come into existence.

The fourth and final model would allow the market decide what works best. For example, there is a belief that Freeports (an onshore low tax zone built around a port) will encourage new R&D businesses to spring up and existing ones to multiply. Although not an investment as such, a softer version of this belief can be seen in R&D Tax Credits, whereby the government foregoes tax revenue to reimburse organisations engaging in R&D activity. Studies by HMRC suggest that for every £1 of tax foregone through a R&D tax credit, between £1.53

and £2.35 additional expenditure by UK companies is stimulated.[13]

The market has not delivered equal outcomes for all areas, and it has not enabled universities to turn the tide of economic inequality. Government has demonstrated in COVID-19 that it can make big public interventions if they believe it is worthwhile or necessary to do so. It will also have to do so in relation to R&D spending. Lining up an articulation of regional strengths, deciding on the most appropriate mechanism, and living up to its promise to resource it could be the way of the government leading an effective post-COVID regional rebalancing, if implemented carefully and with thought. It may be the case that the government has to deploy a number of these tools, or varying tools for varying needs of the places at hand. The starting point for this work should be a conversation with universities and the places they are based, as the institution that can bring all these facets together.

Culture and research

Places must tackle the difficult circumstances they have been dealt, and be supported in doing so. They cannot be allowed to wither, culturally or economically. A recovery without the joys of culture would be moribund, while a cultural recovery without an economic one is impossible. That is why universities are uniquely positioned to facilitate the recovery of place.

Developing distinct regional research strategies helps the resilience of a place. It distinguishes its unique strengths and it forces civic leaders together to decide what is important to the future of their places. In being clear in their priorities universities can be useful partners to their civic stakeholders and help forge economic strategies which change the world.

Combining this with a cultural offer that shares the best of their work while promoting the work of others is not only the morally right thing to do, but the best route to securing their future at a time when government is sceptical of the value of arts education.

Universities are already important to their places. Bringing together a research strategy with a cultural offer will make them indispensable, to even the greatest of sceptics.

Conclusion

The university sector needs as many friends as it can get. The drone that it is not delivering value for money, that it is plagued by 'mickey mouse' degrees, and that it's simply not affordable to send so many people to university, is becoming a chorus. This book is likely coming out around the government's Comprehensive Spending Review and this could upturn many of the assumptions within these pages – it's always the risk of trying to capture a vast and evolving subject. As you read, it could already be the case that funding is eking out of the sector, numbers of students are being restricted, and that slow drip of doubt has become a flood of sector change.

I hope I'm wrong. I hope it goes the other way. The sector tends to wrap itself in a cloak of pessimism even at the best of times. However, if funding and support were to be cut it would of course be a shame for the universities, but it would be a tragedy for the people and the places they were built to serve. The value of universities is so hard to capture precisely because they have so much impact, on so many levels and in so many areas. They are places of education and research, but they are also employers, purchasers, leaders, builders, place makers, volunteer hubs, connectors, advocates, retailers, curators, communities, and they are and can be so much more.

It is simply unimaginable to think what some places would be like without their university. They would suffer an economic loss, but it would be much more than that. It would be a loss of identity, a sense of who they are, and a magnet for some of the things that make places brilliant. It would be a loss of people, of culture, of opportunity and exploration.

The new university, at its heart, is about acknowledging that the world has changed after COVID and that universities have to change as well. Nothing less than a reimagining of stimulating economic activity, expanding the franchise of education, and embedding themselves in place, will anchor them firmly enough to withstand the forces of change that will buffet them. This may be change from government but it is also a threat to their social contract. A university exists in the belief it can make things better for those who attend. If this contract begins to erode, the power of our institutions will as well.

Like the rest of our public institutions, universities face

a major challenge. There is a route through the challenges by adopting a 'business as usual' approach, where those institutions of sufficient reputation and finance continue to grow due to international fees and their reputation. In turn, there will be lots of letters, head shaking, and disappointment as smaller universities are allowed, or perhaps forced, to wilt. Simultaneously, there will be those in between places hoping they last just long enough to avoid the waves of changes crashing upon them and able to keep their head afloat, though not able to fully thrive and service their people and community as they were set up, and aspire, to do. If these institutions were to close it would not only be the economic loss to contend with but a collective failure of ambition and imagination.

I said that the Government's Comprehensive Spending Review could shift a lot of what is laid out in *The New University*. There is a lot to preserve but there is also a moment to grasp. Picture a full reimagining of the scope and possibility of universities to truly shape the future, and benefit those attending and the people and locations that surround it, no matter their background or circumstance. Imagine what the right funding in the right places, and the due importance of sectors like the arts being allowed to thrive, and not cut in favour of one another, could do for communities, to society at large. Imagine taking forward the learnings that have arisen from the pandemic on an accessible education system.

The New University is a proposition of possibility. If the core contract is the belief that a university can make things better for those that attend then there is a new world within our grasp. An approach to place which sees universities as shapers, creators, and investors with and for their local communities. An approach to work where universities are creating jobs, not just supplying the graduates to fill them. A relentless focus on access which warmly embraces blunt tools to crack the hardest and deepest running inequalities. An embrace of culture in all its forms where universities are showing off their best, sharing the work of others, and helping students grow up with their place. And, in partnership with governments, a considered research plan which finds the sweet spot between where investment can make the biggest social and economic difference and builds on existing strengths.

For anyone reading this book, I hope you close it feeling more optimistic. Universities are doing wonderful things and they should be amongst our most treasured assets. The frustration with universities is that they could be better. Better neighbours. Better at getting people in, and getting people moving on. Better integrated with their surroundings and community. And better at bringing success to the places they are based.

Finally, for those of us who believe in the sector, and for those who could believe in the sector as a means of social impact and support, whether now or in a new form, the question is: what next?

If you haven't been to your local university in a while, go and take a look at it. Take your neighbours with you, take your colleagues, take the young people in your life who may never have been to one yet. Take a day trip to your nearest one if there is not one where you live, look around, see what surrounds it, see the life flow of a university in full swing. Go to the student plays where people are learning their craft and ask how more people could enjoy it. Visit your local university museum and wonder what delights exist on your doorstep. Speak to the young people in your life and ask them if they know where the local university is, what it does, and whether they would like to go. Walk into the middle of your town and ask why an institution which shapes, creates, and boosts, local economies does not have a greater presence. The new university is mine and yours, and a gift to the generation that comes after us; cherish it, play a part in nurturing it, watch it grow into a community asset of enormous proportions.

It is up to all of us to build the post-pandemic world we want to live in, to move towards something new, instead of back to how it was before. The new university belongs to all of us and its value is only realised if we engage with it, understand it, and challenge it – push it to be better, for everyone.

References

Introduction

1. "Who's studying in HE?" *HESA*, www.hesa.ac.uk/data-and-analysis/students/whos-in-he. Accessed 17 August 2021.
2. Ibid.
3. "Millennium mothers want university education for their children." *Centre for Longitudinal Studies*, 15 October 2010, cls.ucl.ac.uk/millennium-mothers-want-university-education-for-their-children/. Accessed 17 August 2021.
4. "Where do FTSE chief executives come from?" Katie Allen, *The Guardian*, 1 November 2013. www.theguardian.com/business/interactive/2013/nov/01/ftse-chief-executives-ceo-analysis. Accessed 17 August 2021.
5. stats.oecd.org
6. "QS World University Rankings." www.topuniversities.com/university-rankings/world-university-rankings/2021. Accessed 17 August 2021.
7. "What is the income of HE providers?" *HESA*, www.hesa.ac.uk/data-and-analysis/finances/income. Accessed 17 August 2021.
8. "Higher education in numbers." *Universities UK*, www.universitiesuk.ac.uk/facts-and-stats/Pages/higher-education-data.aspx. Accessed 17 August 2021.
9. "Freedom of Speech (Universities)." Mr David Davis, *UK Parliament*, 19 January 2021. hansard.parliament.uk/commons/2021-01-19/debates/A245BD12-7C20-4D6E-BD87-C73D1ABC6182/FreedomOfSpeech(Universities). Accessed 17 August 2021.
10. "War of the woke! Liz Truss snubs 'fashionable' race and gender focus – 'Tools of the left'." James Bickerton, *Express*,

17 December 2020. www.express.co.uk/news/uk/1373518/
Liz-Truss-news-woke-race-gender-quoters-unconscious-bias-
training-equality-ont. Accessed 17 August 2021.

11. "EMP13: Employment by industry." *Office for National
Statistics*, 17 August 2021. www.ons.gov.uk/employmentand-
labourmarket/peopleinwork/employmentandemployeetypes/
datasets/employmentbyindustryemp13. Accessed 17 August
2021.

12. "Widening Participation in Higher Education, England,
2017/18 age cohort – Official Statistics." *Department for
Education*, assets.publishing.service.gov.uk/government/
uploads/system/uploads/attachment_data/file/852633/
WP2019-MainText.pdf. Accessed 17 August 2021.

Chapter 1: The Crisis of Work

1. "Students more anxious than excited about starting their
careers, despite confidence they will find work." Higher
Education Policy Institute, 28 April 2020. www.hepi.
ac.uk/2020/04/28/students-more-anxious-than-excited-
about-starting-their-careers-despite-confidence-they-will-find-
work/. Accessed 19 August 2021.

2. "The kids aren't alright: How Generation Covid is losing out."
Federica Cocco, *Financial Times*, 17 November 2020.
www.ft.com/content/0dec0291-2f72-4ce9-bd9f-
ae2356bd869e. Accessed 19 August 2021.

3. "Leader's speech, Bournemouth 1999." Tony Blair, *British
Political Speech*. www.britishpoliticalspeech.org/speech-ar-
chive.htm?speech=205. Accessed 21 August 2021.

4. "Chris Skidmore: Why it's time to ditch the 50 per cent
target for universities." Chris Skidmore, *Conservative Home*,
9 July 2020. www.conservativehome.com/platform/2020/07/
chris-skidmore-why-its-time-to-ditch-the-50-per-cent-target-
for-universities.html. Accessed 21 August 2021.

5. "Blair's university drive is real reason behind HGV drivers
shortage – Andrew Bridgen." David Williamson, *Express*,
31 July 2021. www.express.co.uk/news/politics/1470465/

HGV-driver-shortage-Tony-Blair-university-andrew-bridgen. Accessed 21 August 2021.

6. "Graduate labour market statistics." *gov.uk*, 10 June 2021. explore-education-statistics.service.gov.uk/find-statistics/graduate-labour-markets. Accessed 21 August 2021.

7. "Graduates' salaries." *HESA*. www.hesa.ac.uk/data-and-analysis/graduates/salaries. Accessed 21 August 2021.

8. "Qualified for the Future." *The British Academy*, May 2020. www.thebritishacademy.ac.uk/documents/1888/Qualified-for-the-Future-Quantifying-demand-for-arts-humanities-social-science-skills.pdf. Accessed 21 August 2021.

9. "ISC Annual Census 2021." *Independent Schools Council*. www.isc.co.uk/media/7491/isc_census_2021.pdf. Accessed 21 August 2021.

10. "Higher education student numbers." Paul Bolton, *House of Commons Library*, 26 February 2021. researchbriefings. files.parliament.uk/documents/CBP-7857/CBP-7857.pdf. Accessed 21 August 2021.

11. "The 2008 recession 10 years on." *Office for National Statistics*, 30 April 2018. www.ons.gov.uk/economy/grossdomesticproductgdp/articles/the2008recession10yearson/2018-04-30. Accessed 21 August 2021.

12. "Average UK wages top pre-financial crisis levels." Richard Partington, *The Guardian*, 18 February 2020. www.theguardian.com/business/2020/feb/18/average-uk-wages-rise-above-pre-financial-crisis-levels. Accessed 21 August 2021.

13. "Coronavirus: Impact on the labour market." Andrew Powell & Brigid Francis-Devine, *House of Commons Library*, 19 August 2021. https://researchbriefings.files.parliament.uk/documents/CBP-8898/CBP-8898.pdf. Accessed 21 August 2021.

14. "Class of 2020: Education leavers in the current crisis." Kathleen Henehan, *Resolution Foundation*, May 2020. www.resolutionfoundation.org/app/uploads/2020/05/Class-of-2020.pdf. Accessed 21 August 2021.

15. Ibid.

16. Ibid.

17. "Youth Unemployment Statistics." Andrew Powell & Brigid

Francis-Devine, *House of Commons Library*, 17 August 2021. researchbriefings.files.parliament.uk/documents/SN05871/ SN05871.pdf. Accessed 21 August 2021.

18. "COVID-19 and Youth Employment." *The Prince's Responsible Business Network*. www.bitc.org.uk/wp-content/ uploads/2020/07/bitc-factsheet-employment-covid19an-dyouthemployment-june20.pdf. Accessed 21 August 2021.

19. "Growing Pains." Stephen Clarke, *Resolution Foundation*, May 2019. www.resolutionfoundation.org/app/uploads/2019/05/ Growing-pains-final-report.pdf. Accessed 21 August 2021.

20. "COVID-19 and Social Mobility Impact Brief #5: Graduate Recruitment and Access to the Workplace." Erica Holt-White & Rebecca Montacute, *The Sutton Trust*, July 2020. www. suttontrust.com/wp-content/uploads/2020/07/Access-to-the-Workplace-Impact-Brief.pdf. Accessed 21 August 2021.

21. "More than half of final year students lose jobs or internships during pandemic." *Prospects*, May 2020. www.prospects. ac.uk/prospects-press-office/more-than-half-of-final-year-students-lose-jobs. Accessed 21 August 2021.

22. "The future of pandemic support for households." Jonathan Cribb, *IFS*, 16 February 2021. ifs.org.uk/uploads/The-future-of-pandemic-support-for-households.pdf. Accessed 21 August 2021.

23. "Percentage of employed graduates in non-graduate roles, parts of the UK, 2015 to 2017." *Office of National Statistics*, 26 April 2018. www.ons.gov.uk/employmentandlabour-market/peopleinwork/employmentandemployeetypes/ adhocs/008381percentageofemployedgraduatesinnongradua-terolespartsoftheuk2015to2017. Accessed 21 August 2021.

24. "A bad time to graduate." Paul Johnson, *IFS*, 17 April 2020. ifs.org.uk/publications/14816. Accessed 21 August 2021.

25. "Where in the UK are you most likely to get a job?" *Target Jobs*. targetjobs.co.uk/careers-advice/career-planning/324633-where-in-the-uk-are-you-most-likely-to-get-a-graduate-job. Accessed 21 August 2021.

26. "The Great British Brain Drain." Paul Swinney & Maire Williams, *Centre for Cities*, November 2016. www.centreforcities. org/wp-content/uploads/2016/11/16-11-18-The-Great-Brit-

ish-Brain-Drain.pdf. Accessed 21 August 2021.

27.   "'The jobs aren't there': why graduates are leaving northern towns." Rachel Hall, *The Guardian*, 16 May 2019. www. theguardian.com/education/2019/may/16/the-jobs-arent-there-why-graduates-are-leaving-northern-towns. Accessed 21 August 2021.

28.   "Jobs lost, jobs gained: What the future of work will mean for jobs, skills, and wages." McKinsey Global Institute, *McKinsey & Company*, 28 November 2017. www.mckinsey.com/featured-insights/future-of-work/jobs-lost-jobs-gained-what-the-future-of-work-will-mean-for-jobs-skills-and-wages. Accessed 21 August 2021.

29.   "Purchase of Debenhams building puts University of Gloucestershire growth plans at heart of city regeneration." *University of Gloucestershire*. www.glos.ac.uk/content/debenhams-building/. Accessed 21 August 2021.

30.   "What is Preston Model?." *Preston City Council*. www.preston. gov.uk/article/1339/What-is-Preston-Model-. Accessed 21 August 2021.

31.   "Truly Civic: Strengthening the connection between universities and their places." *UPP Foundation*. upp-foundation. org/wp-content/uploads/2019/02/Civic-University-Commission-Final-Report.pdf. Accessed 21 August 2021.

32.   "What is Community Wealth Building?" *CLES*. cles. org.uk/community-wealth-building/what-is-community-wealth-building/. Accessed 21 August 2021.

33.   "It's time universities made the most of their purchasing power." Nick Petford, The Guardian, 2 July 2012. www. theguardian.com/higher-education-network/blog/2012/jul/02/procurement-in-universities. Accessed 21 August 2021.

34.   "From the garage to the Googleplex." *Google*. about.google/ our-story/. Accessed 21 August 2021.

35.   "10 standout university spinouts." Glyn Mon Hughes, *University Business*, 15 March 2021. universitybusiness.co.uk/features/10-standout-university-spinouts/. Accessed 21 August 2021.

36.   "#C21stLab." *University of Lincoln*. 21stcenturylab.lincoln. ac.uk/. Accessed 21 August 2021.

Chapter 2: The Crisis of Opportunity

1. For example: "It's time for bursaries to demonstrate their impact." Les Ebdon, *Wonkhe*, 5 December 2016. wonkhe. com/blogs/its-time-for-bursaries-to-demonstrate-real-impact/. Accessed 21 August 2021.
2. "Fees and funding." *LSE*. www.lse.ac.uk/study-at-lse/Undergraduate/fees-and-funding. Accessed 21 August 2021.
3. "Student loan statistics." Paul Bolton, *House of Commons Library*, 23 June 2021. commonslibrary.parliament.uk/ research-briefings/sn01079/. Accessed 21 August 2021.
4. "Student loan forecasts for England." *gov.uk*, 24 September 2020, explore-education-statistics.service.gov.uk/find-statistics/student-loan-forecasts-for-england/2019-20#releaseHeadlines-summary
5. "Understanding costs of undergraduate provision in Higher Education." *KPMG LLP*, Department for Education, May 2019. assets.publishing.service.gov.uk/government/uploads/ system/uploads/attachment_data/file/909349/Understanding_costs_of_undergraduate_provision_in_higher_education. pdf. Accessed 21 August 2021.
6. "2021 cycle applicant figures – January equal consideration deadline." *UCAS*, www.ucas.com/data-and-analysis/undergraduate-statistics-and-reports/ucas-undergraduate-releases/ applicant-releases-2021/2021-cycle-applicant-figures-january-deadline?hash=brm-l3o_APNzR38bJPg4F2VfBCXapfK-ACKkXGdogwFo. Accessed 21 August 2021.
7. "How UK universities will attract international students in 2021-22." *Study International*, 14 July 2021. www.study-international.com/news/uk-universities-idp-andy-howell/. Accessed 21 August 2021.
8. "Too many students take courses that don't benefit them or the economy." Paul Johnson, *IFS*, 2 March 2020. https://ifs. org.uk/publications/14741. Accessed 21 August 2021.
9. "Shaping higher education." *LSE*. http://wwww.lse.ac.uk/ economics/Assets/Documents/50YearsAfterRobbins.pdf. Accessed 21 August 2021.

10. "Further and Higher Education Act 1992." *legislation.gov.uk*. www.legislation.gov.uk/ukpga/1992/13/contents. Accessed 21 August 2021.

11. "The Browne report: higher education funding and student finance." *gov.uk*, 12 October 2010. www.gov.uk/government/publications/the-browne-report-higher-education-funding-and-student-finance. Accessed 21 August 2021.

12. "Higher education student numbers." Paul Bolton, *House of Commons Library*, 26 February 2021. researchbriefings.files.parliament.uk/documents/CBP-7857/CBP-7857.pdf. Accessed 21 August 2021.

13. Ibid.

14. "Who's studying in HE?" *HESA*, www.hesa.ac.uk/data-and-analysis/students/whos-in-he. Accessed 21 August 2021.

15. "Where do HE students come from?" *HESA*, www.hesa.ac.uk/data-and-analysis/students/whos-in-he. Accessed 21 August 2021.

16. "Higher education student numbers." Paul Bolton, *House of Commons Library*, 26 February 2021. researchbriefings.files.parliament.uk/documents/CBP-7857/CBP-7857.pdf. Accessed 21 August 2021.

17. "Widening participation in higher education." *gov.uk*, 30 July 2020. explore-education-statistics.service.gov.uk/find-statistics/widening-participation-in-higher-education#dataBlock-1df1eed7-3f0c-458e-a135-08d821b65a1f-charts. Accessed 21 August 2021.

18. "Entry rates into higher education." *gov.uk*, 16 February 2021. www.ethnicity-facts-figures.service.gov.uk/education-skills-and-training/higher-education/entry-rates-in-to-higher-education/latest. Accessed 21 August 2021.

19. "Undergraduate degree results." *gov.uk*, 2 August 2021. https://www.ethnicity-facts-figures.service.gov.uk/education-skills-and-training/higher-education/undergraduate-degree-results/latest. Accessed 21 August 2021.

20. "Destinations and earnings of graduates after higher education." *gov.uk*, 18 December 2020. www.ethnicity-facts-figures.service.gov.uk/education-skills-and-training/after-education/

destinations-and-earnings-of-graduates-after-higher-educa-tion/latest. 21 August 2021.

21. "Graduate outcomes (LEO): Employment and earnings outcomes of higher education graduates by subject studied and graduate characteristics in 2016/17." *Department for Education*, 28 March 2019. assets.publishing.service.gov.uk/government/uploads/system/uploads/attachment_data/file/790223/Main_text.pdf. Accessed 21 August 2021.

22. "Too many students take courses that don't benefit them or the economy." Paul Johnson, *IFS*, 2 March 2020. ifs.org.uk/publications/14741. Accessed 21 August 2021.

23. "Children are being sidelined by covid-19." *BMJ*, 27 May 2020. www.bmj.com/content/369/bmj.m2061. Accessed 21 August 2021.

24. "Enterprise Zones." Matthew Ward, *House of Commons Library*, 21 January 2020. commonslibrary.parliament.uk/research-briefings/sn05942/. Accessed 21 August 2021.

25. "What happened to the COVID cohort?" *UCAS*. www.ucas.com/file/411836/download?token=51eovdPq. Accessed 21 August 2021.

26. "Summer 2020 outcomes did not systemically disadvantage students." *gov.uk*, 26 November 2020. www.gov.uk/government/news/summer-2020-outcomes-did-not-systemically-dis-advantage-students. Accessed 21 August 2021.

27. "UCAS undergraduate sector-level end of cycle data resources 2020." *UCAS*, www.ucas.com/data-and-analysis/undergrad-uate-statistics-and-reports/ucas-undergraduate-sector-lev-el-end-cycle-data-resources-2020. Accessed 21 August 2021.

28. "Level 2 and 3 attainment by young people aged 19." *gov.uk*, 29 April 2021. explore-education-statistics.service.gov.uk/find-statistics/level-2-and-3-attainment-by-young-peo-ple-aged-19/2019-20#releaseHeadlines-charts. Accessed 21 August 2021.

29. "Preparing for degree study." *Office for Students*, 13 May 2019. www.officeforstudents.org.uk/media/f3450e04-2d2b-4b33-932f-41140d57c41e/ofs2019_20.pdf. Accessed 21 August 2021.

30. "Review of Post-18 Education and Funding." *gov.uk*, May

2019. assets.publishing.service.gov.uk/government/uploads/system/uploads/attachment_data/file/805127/Review_of_post_18_education_and_funding.pdf. Accessed 21 August 2021.

31. "Year 0: A foundation for widening participation?" *HESA*, 16 May 2019. www.hesa.ac.uk/blog/16-05-2019/foundation-year-research, Accessed 21 August 2021.

32. "Progression from the Foundation Year." *LMH*. www.lmh.ox.ac.uk/prospective-students/foundation-year/lmh-foundation-year-students/studying-foundation-year-1. Accessed 21 August 2021.

33. "Year 0: A foundation for widening participation?" *HESA*, 16 May 2019. www.hesa.ac.uk/blog/16-05-2019/foundation-year-research, Accessed 21 August 2021.

34. "Poorer children's educational attainment: how imortant are attitudes and behaviour?" Alissa Goodman & Paul Gregg, *Joseph Rowntree Foundation*, March 2010. www.jrf.org.uk/sites/default/files/jrf/migrated/files/poorer-children-education-full.pdf. Accessed 21 August 2021.

35. "GCSE results: the hidden but enduring effects of parental social class." *LSE*, 20 August 2020. blogs.lse.ac.uk/politicsandpolicy/gcse-results-parental-social-class/. Accessed 21 August 2021.

36. "Early-in-Year Student Withdrawal Notifications." *Student Loans Company*. assets.publishing.service.gov.uk/government/uploads/system/uploads/attachment_data/file/968409/EIY_Notifications_of_Student_Withdrawals_-_AY20201_Feb21.pdf. Accessed 21 August 2021.

37. "Predicted grades: accuracy and impact." Dr Gill Wyness, *UCL*, December 2016. www.ucu.org.uk/media/8409/Predicted-grades-accuracy-and-impact-Dec-16/pdf/Predicted_grades_report_Dec2016.pdf. Accessed 21 August 2021.

38. "Predicting A-level grades accurately 'near-impossible task'." *UCL*, 11 August 2020. www.ucl.ac.uk/news/2020/aug/predicting-level-grades-accurately-near-impossible-task. Accessed 21 August 2021.

39. "Contextual admissions." *Office for Students*, 27 July 2020. www.officeforstudents.org.uk/advice-and-guidance/promot-

ing-equal-opportunities/effective-practice/contextual-admis-
sions/. Accessed 21 August 2021.

40. "Academic entry explained." *University of St Andews.* www.
st-andrews.ac.uk/subjects/entry/academic-entry-explained/.
Accessed 21 August 2021.

41. "Admissions schemes." *Imperial College London.* www.
imperial.ac.uk/study/ug/apply/selection/admissions-schemes/.
Accessed 21 August 2021.

42. "Adjusted entry requirements and contextual admissions."
University of Glasgow. www.gla.ac.uk/study/wp/adjust-
edoffers/. Accessed 21 August 2021.

43. "Who's studying in HE?" *HESA,* www.hesa.ac.uk/
data-and-analysis/students/whos-in-he. Accessed 21 August
2021.

44. "Bursaries are an important component of widening participation in Higher Education and their funding should
be maintained." *University of Bristol.* www.bristol.ac.uk/
media-library/sites/sraa/documents/Policy%20Briefing%20
Harris_bursaries%20Final.pdf. Accessed 21 August 2021.

45. Llie, S. Horner, A. Kaye, N. and Curran, S. (2019). Financial
Support and Undergraduate Outcomes in the University of
Cambridge. University of Cambridge Faculty of Education, p
1-63.

46. "Do student bursaries work? Help me find out." Vanessa
Todman, *King's College London,* 6 January 2020. www.kcl.
ac.uk/news/do-student-bursaries-work-help-me-find-out.
Accessed 21 August 2021.

Chapter 3: The Crisis of Place

1. "Coronavirus and vaccine attitudes and behaviours in England:
over 80s population, 15 February to 20 February 2021." Kath-
ryn Littleboy, *Office for National Statistics,* 4 March 2021. www.
ons.gov.uk/peoplepopulationandcommunity/healthandsocial-
care/conditionsanddiseases/bulletins/coronavirusandvaccineat-
titudesandbehavioursinengland/over80spopulation15february-
to20february2021. Accessed 21 August 2021.

2. www.theyworkforyou.com/debates/?id=2021-03-09b.649.3

&s=Milton+Keynes+University#g653.2. Accessed 21 August 2021.

3. "Religion." *The National Centre for Social Research*. www.bsa. natcen.ac.uk/media/39293/1_bsa36_religion.pdf. Accessed 21 August 2021.

4. "Introduction: the lie of the land." *Land for the Many*. land-forthemany.uk/introduction-the-lie-of-the-land/. Accessed 21 August 2021.

5. "Report on the use of Zero Hour Contracts." Ernestine Gheyoh Ndzi, Janet Barlow, Steve Shelley & Jane Hardy, *University of Hertfordshire*, July 2017. researchprofiles.herts.ac.uk/portal/files/12097546/Report.pdf. Accessed 21 August 2021.

6. "Culture at home." *University of Liverpool*. www.liverpool. ac.uk/coronavirus/culture/. Accessed 21 August 2021.

7. www.mercury92.com/AU-Museums/Egypt.html. Accessed 21 August 2021.

8. "Reflecting on Covid-19's Impact on Arts, Culture and Heritage." *University of Leeds*. ahc.leeds.ac.uk/fine-art/events/event/2175/reflecting-on-covid-19-s-impact-on-arts-culture-and-heritage. Accessed 21 August 2021.

9. "Ancient Mariner Big Read." *University of Plymouth*. www. plymouth.ac.uk/students-and-family/arts-institute-public-programme/big-read. 21 August 2021.

10. "Extraordinary year sees annual art exhibition shift online." *University of Cumbria*. www.cumbria.ac.uk/about/news/articles/articles/extraordinary-year-sees-annual-art-exhibition-shift-online.html. Accessed 21 August 2021.

11. "Level 5 Show 2021." *University of Brighton*. blogs.brighton. ac.uk/l5show2021/category/all-shows/. Accessed 21 August 2021.

12. "Impact and Engagement." *University Museums Group*. universitymuseumsgroup.org/wp-content/uploads/2013/11/UMG-ADVOCACY-single.pdf. Accessed 21 August 2021.

13. "Culture shock: COVID-19 and the cultural and creative sectors." *OECD*, 7 September 2020. www.oecd.org/coronavirus/policy-responses/culture-shock-covid-19-and-the-cultural-and-creative-sectors-08da9e0e/. Accessed 21 August 2021.

14. "Gavin Williamson: Skills, jobs and freedom. My priori-

ties for this week's Queen's Speech – and the year ahead." Gavin Williamson, *Conservative Home*, 14 May 2021. www. conservativehome.com/platform/2021/05/gavin-williamson-skills-jobs-and-freedom-my-priorities-for-this-weeks-queens-speech-and-the-year-ahead.html. Accessed 21 August 2021.

15. "Qualified for the Future." *The British Academy*, May 2020. www.thebritishacademy.ac.uk/documents/1888/Quali-fied-for-the-Future-Quantifying-demand-for-arts-human-ities-social-science-skills.pdf. Accessed 21 August 2021.

Chapter 4: The Crisis of Relevance

1. "A Call to Stop the Next Pandemic." *WWF*. www.worldwild-life.org/stories/a-call-to-stop-the-next-pandemic. Accessed 21 August 2021.

2. "Harold Wilson's 'white heat of technology' speech 50 years on." Matthew Francis, *The Guardian*, 19 September 2013. www.theguardian.com/science/political-science/2013/sep/19/harold-wilson-white-heat-technology-speech. Accessed 21 August 2021.

3. "Research and development spending." Chris Rhodes, Georgina Hutton & Matthew Ward, *House of Commons Library*, 16 March 2021. commonslibrary.parliament.uk/research-briefings/sn04223/. Accessed 21 August 2021.

4. "Research & Development spending." Chris Rhodes & Matthew Ward, *House of Commons Library*, 16 March 2021. researchbriefings.files.parliament.uk/documents/SN04223/SN04223.pdf. Accessed 21 August 2021.

5. Ibid.

6. "Levelling Up Innovation: Boosting R&D in Underper-forming Regions." Bill Wildi, *Tony Blair Institute for Global Change*, 14 September 2020. institute.global/policy/lev-elling-innovation-boosting-rd-underperforming-regions. Accessed 21 August 2021.

7. "Spending Review 2020." *gov.uk*, November 2020. assets.pub-lishing.service.gov.uk/government/uploads/system/uploads/attachment_data/file/938054/SR20_print.pdf. Accessed 21 August 2021.

8. qna.files.parliament.uk/qna-attachments/1135062/original/ HL16689_UK_Research_and_Innovation_Report.pdf. Accessed 21 August 2021.
9. csconnected.com/. Accessed 21 August 2021.
10. "About us." *GOFCoE*. www.globalopenfinance.com/ about-us/. Accessed 21 August 2021.
11. "MyWorld." *University of Bristol*. www.bristol.ac.uk/vision-in-stitute/myworld/. Accessed 21 August 2021.
12. "The Missing £4 Billion." *Nesta*, 27 May 2020. www.nesta. org.uk/report/the-missing-4-billion/. Accessed 21 August 2021.
13. "Evaluation of Researcg ad Development Tax Credit." *HM Revenue & Customs*, March 2015. assets.publishing.service. gov.uk/government/uploads/system/uploads/attachment_ data/file/413629/HMRC_WorkingPaper_17_R_D_Evaluation_Final.pdf. Accessed 21 August 2021.

Acknowledgements

Thanks are owed to Debbie McVitty at WonkHE, Anne-Marie Canning at The Brilliant Club, Diana Beech at London Higher, Nick Hillman at HEPI, Dean Machin at the University of Portsmouth, and Professor Dame Janet Beer and John Corish at the University of Liverpool, for sharing their ideas with me in writing this book. Thanks also go to Jarvis (my cat) for the company in the long nights of typing.

I owe an enormous debt of gratitude to Professor Dinah Birch for not only being a wonderful colleague but a patient and kind reviewer of earlier drafts of *The New University*.

Any errors remain my own.

About the Author

James Coe works as the senior policy advisor at the University of Liverpool, and is studying for a Masters in Public Administration at the University of York. He is interested in the capacity of the public sector to transform the lives of all of those who come into contact with it, developed over years working in the charity and higher education sectors.

About the Author

About the Inklings series

This book is part of 404 Ink's Inkling series which presents big ideas in pocket-sized books.
They are all available at 404ink.com/shop

If you enjoyed this book, you may also enjoy these titles in the series:

The Appendix: Transmasculine Joy in a Transphobic Culture – Liam Konemann

 In 2019, Liam Konemann began collating what he called 'The Appendix', a simple record of ongoing transphobia in the UK that he came across in day-to-day life: from the flippant comments of peers to calculated articles and reviews in newspapers. When the list began to take its toll on his mental health, he changed tack by asking different questions: how is beauty in transmasculinity found? And how is it maintained in a transphobic world?

Blind Spot: Exploring and Educating on Blindness – Maud Rowell

When it comes to blindness, people can often have many questions and few answers. In *Blind Spot*, Maud educates about the realities of living with sight loss, offering the knowledge they need to become better, more tolerant members of diverse communities.

No Man's Land: Living Between Two Cultures – Anne East

In *No Man's Land*, Anne explores this chasm in more detail, how it is to feel one thing and yet be perceived as another. What are the emotions that people feel in this limbo? Why is culture so important? And how does it feel to experience that cultural no man's land? A book on acceptance and shining a light on the cultural vacuum that exists for many, this is a must read from a voice rarely heard.